FOR ORGANS, PIANOS & ELECTRONIC KEYBOARDS

E-Z PLAY® TODAY

136

Disney® FUN SONGS

ISBN 978-1-5400-4934-6

The following songs are the property of:

Bourne Co.
Music Publishers
5 West 37th Street
New York, NY 10018

GIVE A LITTLE WHISTLE
HEIGH-HO
I'VE GOT NO STRINGS
WHEN I SEE AN ELEPHANT FLY
WHISTLE WHILE YOU WORK
WHO'S AFRAID OF THE BIG BAD WOLF?

Visit Hal Leonard Online at
www.halleonard.com

Contact us:
Hal Leonard
7777 West Bluemound Road
Milwaukee, WI 53213
Email: info@halleonard.com

In Europe, contact:
Hal Leonard Europe Limited
42 Wigmore Street
Marylebone, London, W1U 2RN
Email: info@halleonardeurope.com

In Australia, contact:
Hal Leonard Australia Pty. Ltd.
4 Lentara Court
Cheltenham, Victoria, 3192 Australia
Email: info@halleonard.com.au

CONTENTS

*Based on the "Winnie the Pooh" works,
by A. A. Milne and E. H. Shepard

The Bare Necessities
from THE JUNGLE BOOK

Registration 4
Rhythm: Fox Trot or Swing

Words and Music by
Terry Gilkyson

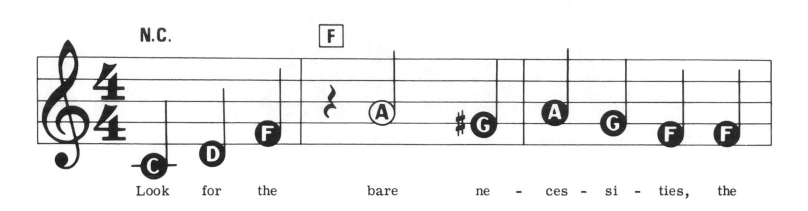

Look for the bare ne - ces - si - ties, the

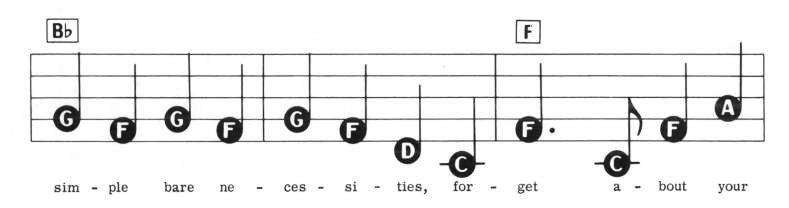

sim - ple bare ne - ces - si - ties, for - get a - bout your

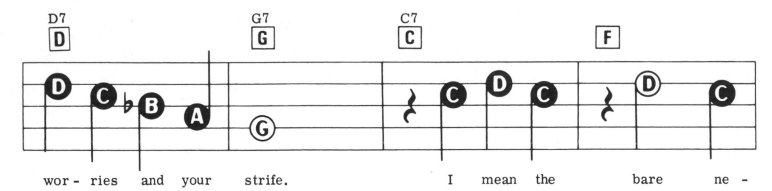

wor - ries and your strife. I mean the bare ne -

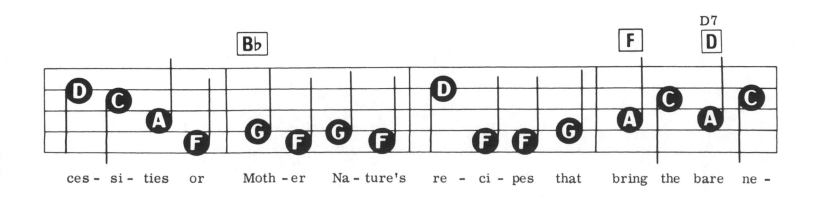

ces - si - ties or Moth - er Na - ture's re - ci - pes that bring the bare ne -

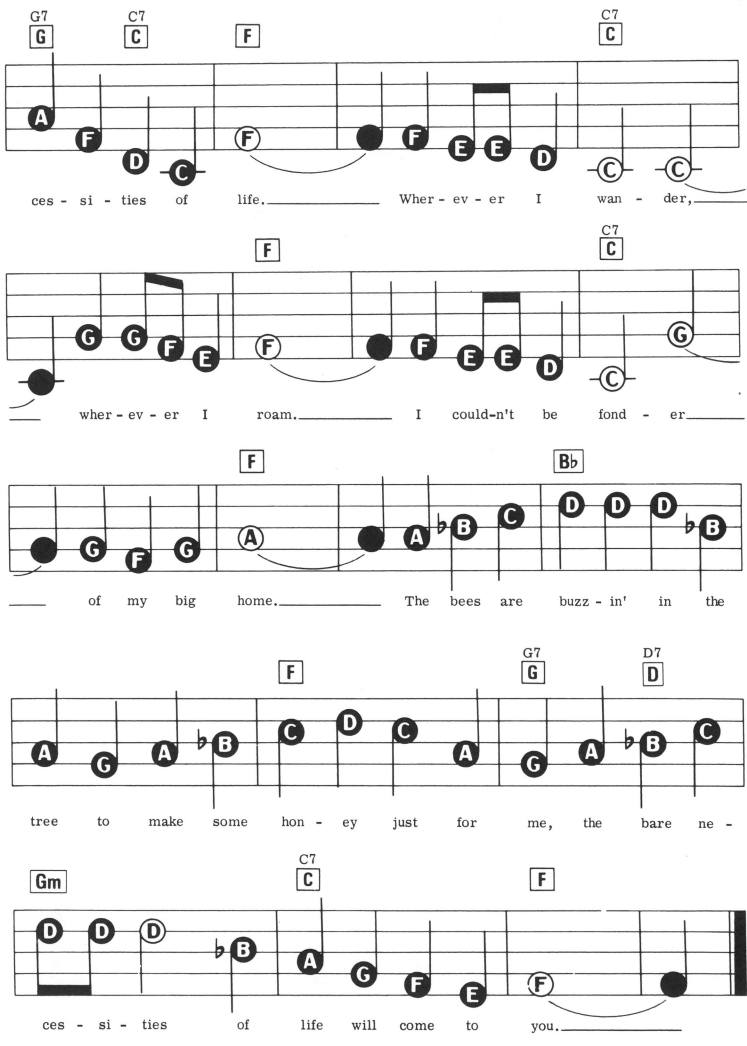

Be Our Guest
from BEAUTY AND THE BEAST

Registration 5
Rhythm: March or Polka

Music by Alan Menken
Lyrics by Howard Ashman

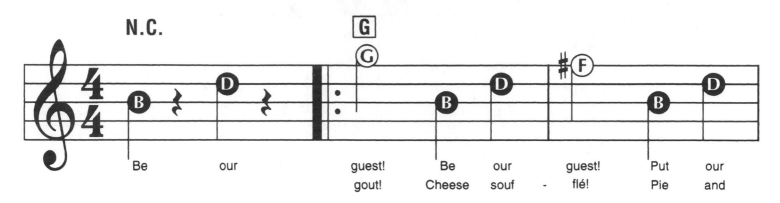

Be our guest! Be our guest! Put our
gout! Cheese souf - flé! Pie and

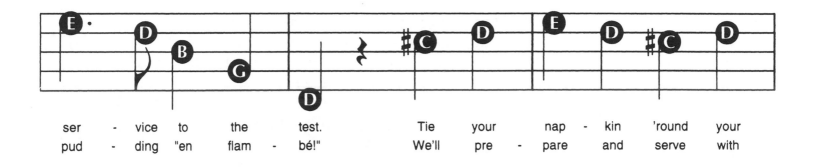

ser - vice to the test. Tie your nap - kin 'round your
pud - ding "en flam - bé!" We'll pre - pare and serve with

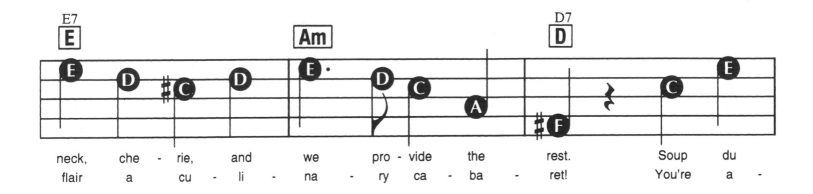

neck, che - rie, and we pro - vide the rest. Soup du
flair a cu - li - na - ry ca - ba - ret! You're a -

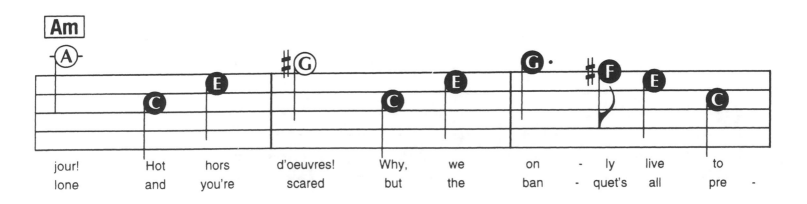

jour! Hot hors d'oeuvres! Why, we on - ly live to
lone and you're scared but the ban - quet's all pre -

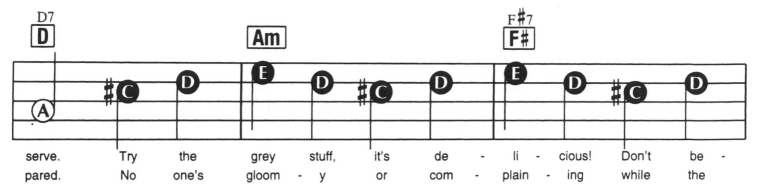

serve. Try the grey stuff, it's de - li - cious! Don't be -
pared. No one's gloom - y or com - plain - ing while the

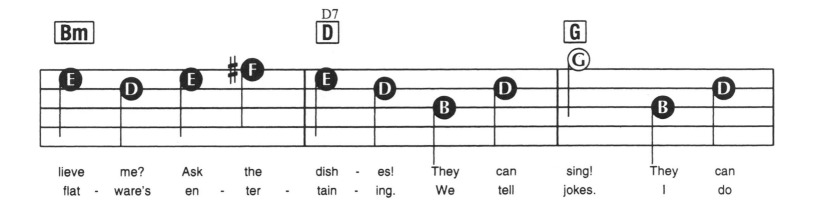

lieve me? Ask the dish - es! They can sing! They can
flat - ware's en - ter - tain - ing. We can tell jokes. I do

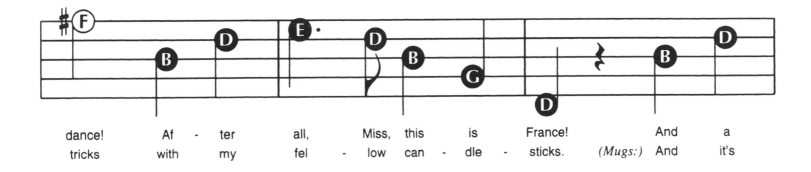

dance! Af - ter all, Miss, this is France! And a
tricks with my fel - low can - dle - sticks. *(Mugs:)* And it's

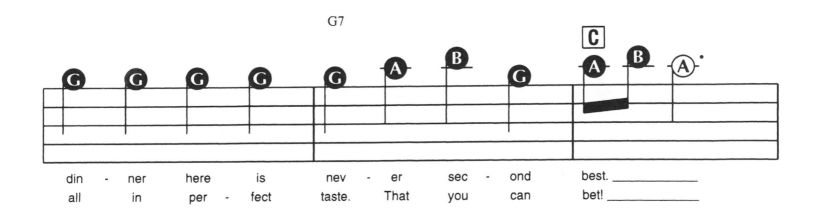

din - ner here is nev - er sec - ond best. _____
all in per - fect taste. That you can bet! _____

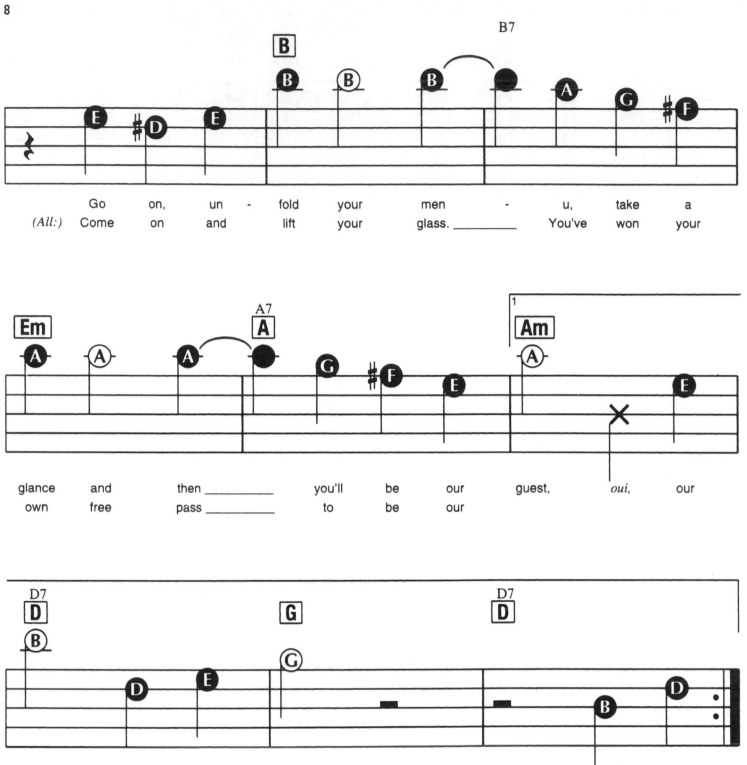

Go on, un - fold your men - u, take a
(All:) Come on and lift your glass. _____ You've won your

glance and then _____ you'll be our guest, *oui,* our
own and free pass _____ to be our

guest! Be our guest! Beef ra -

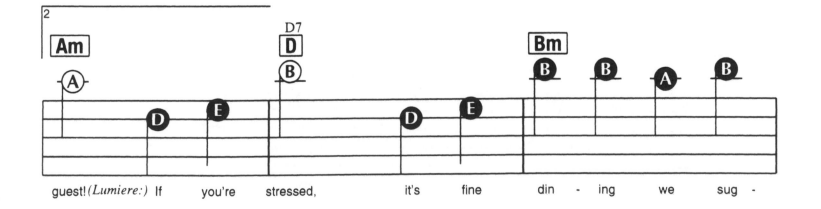

guest! (Lumiere:) If you're stressed, it's fine din - ing we sug -

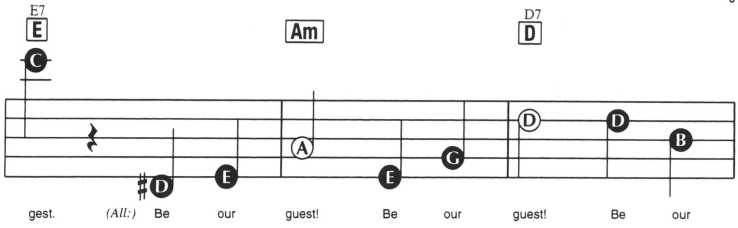

gest. *(All:)* Be our guest! Be our guest! Be our

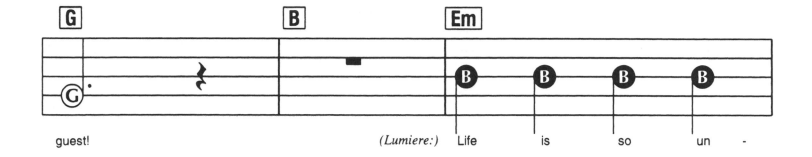

guest! *(Lumiere:)* Life is so un -

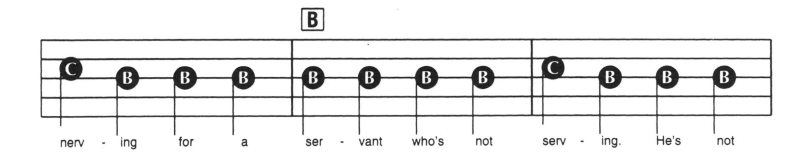

nerv - ing for a ser - vant who's not serv - ing. He's not

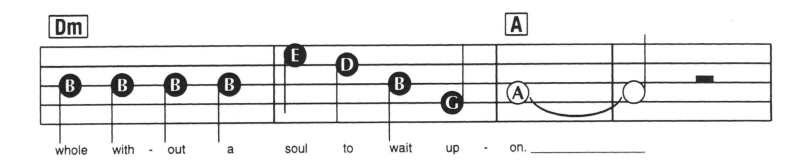

whole with - out a soul to wait up - on. _____

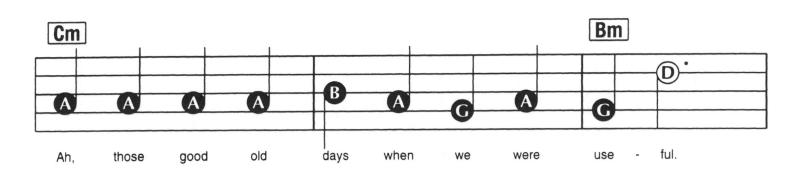

Ah, those good old days when we were use - ful.

Em   **Am**

C C C B A B C A

Sud - den - ly, those good old days are

B7
B   **Em**

B G G G G

gone.   *(Spoken:) Ten*   *years,*   *we've*   *been*

B

G G G G #F #F #F #F #F #F #F #F

rust - ing,   *need - ing*   *so*   *much*   *more*   *than*   *dust - ing. Need - ing*

Dm   **A**

F F F. F F. F F F E

ex - er - cise,   *a*   *chance*   *to*   *use*   *our*   *skills.*

Cm

A A A A B A G A

Most days, we just lay a - round the

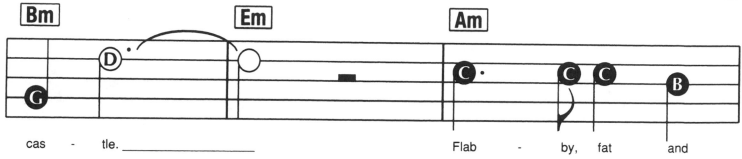

cas - tle. _____ Flab - by, fat and

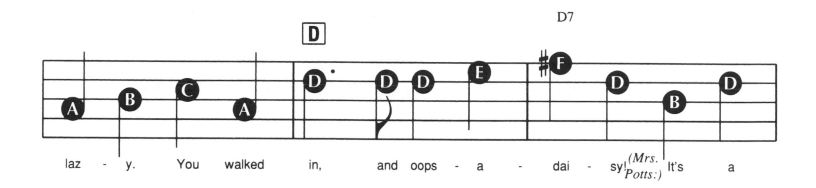

laz - y. You walked in, and oops - a - dai - sy! *(Mrs. Potts:)* It's a

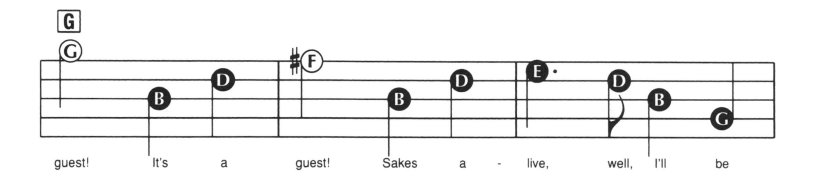

guest! It's a guest! Sakes a - live, well, I'll be

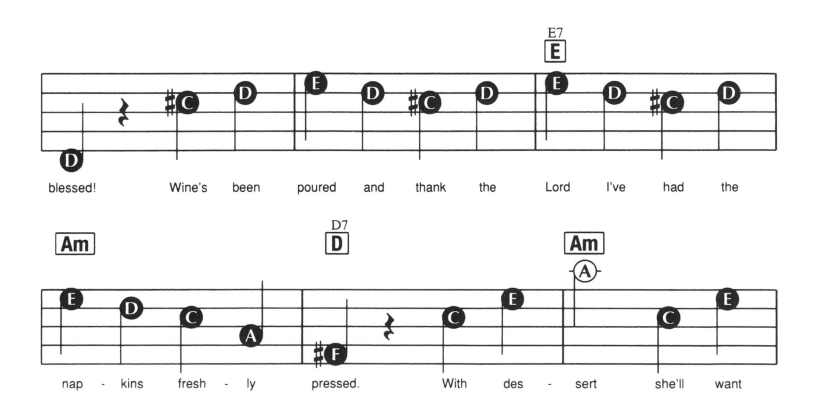

blessed! Wine's been poured and thank the Lord I've had the

nap - kins fresh - ly pressed. With des - sert she'll want

tea. And my dear, that's fine with me. While the

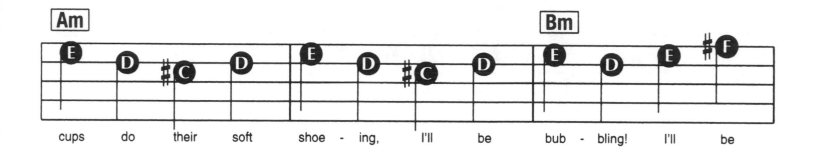

cups do their soft shoe - ing, I'll be bub - bling! I'll be

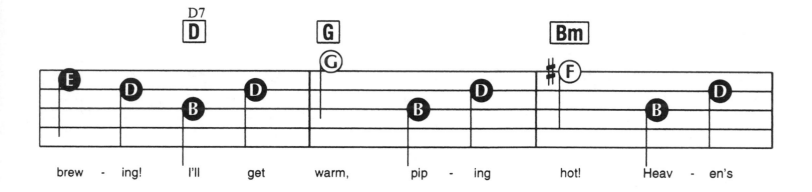

brew - ing! I'll get warm, pip - ing hot! Heav - en's

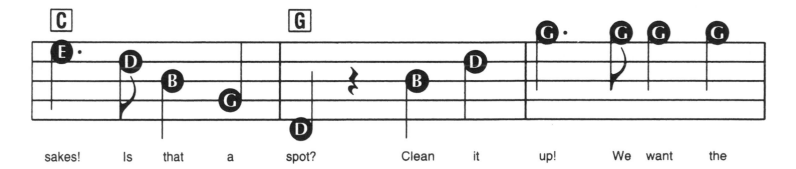

sakes! Is that a spot? Clean it up! We want the

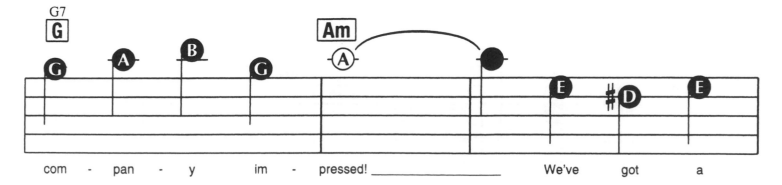

com - pan - y im - pressed! _____ We've got a

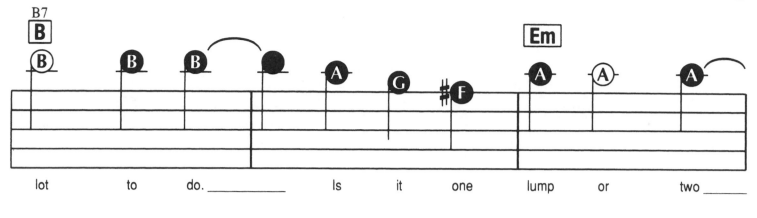

lot to do. _____ Is it one lump or two _____

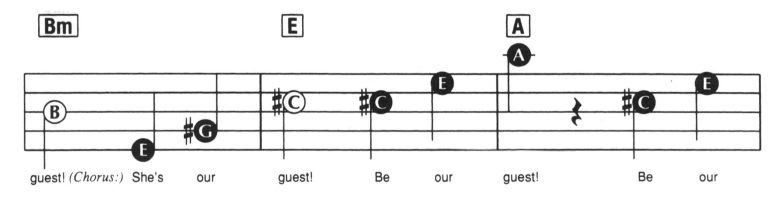

_____ for you, our guest? *(Chorus:)* She's our guest! *(Mrs. Potts:)* She's our

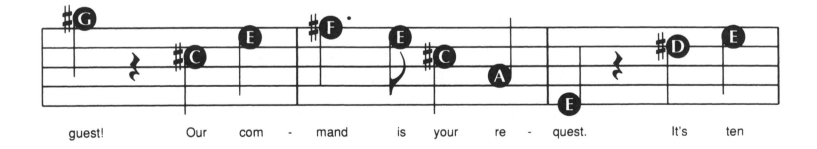

guest! *(Chorus:)* She's our guest! Be our guest! Be our

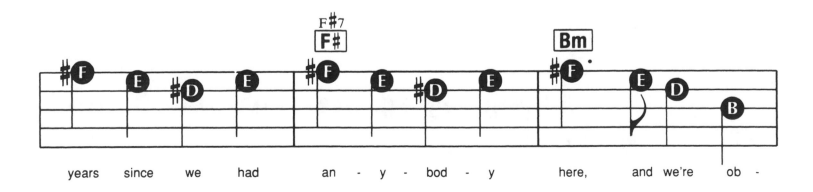

guest! Our com - mand is your re - quest. It's ten

years since we had an - y - bod - y here, and we're ob -

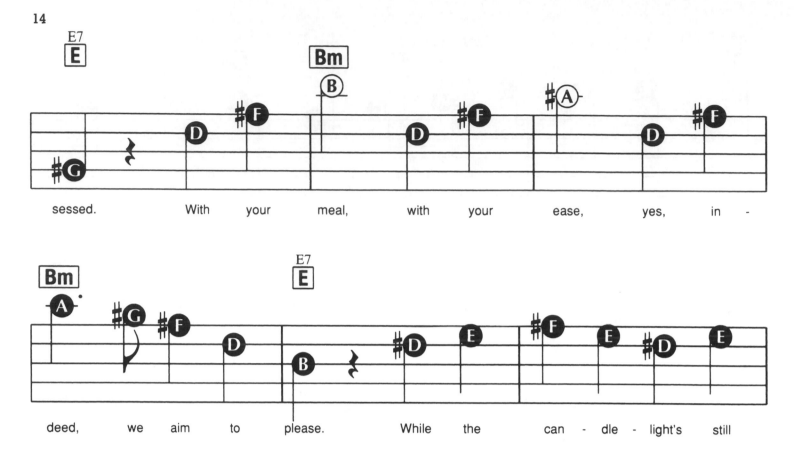

sessed. With your meal, with your ease, yes, in -

deed, we aim to please. While the can - dle - light's still

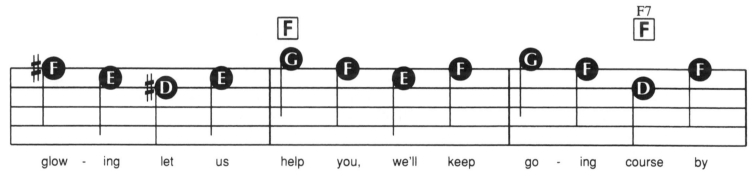

glow - ing let us help you, we'll keep go - ing course by

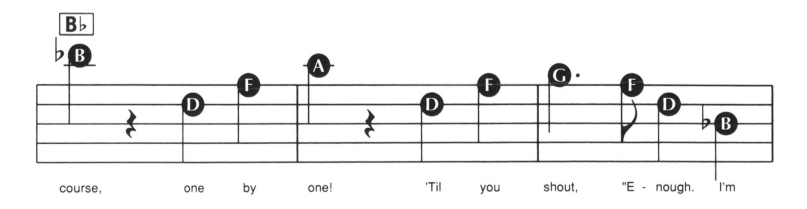

course, one by one! 'Til you shout, "E - nough. I'm

B♭7

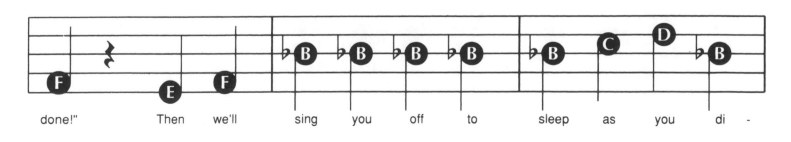

done!" Then we'll sing you off to sleep as you di -

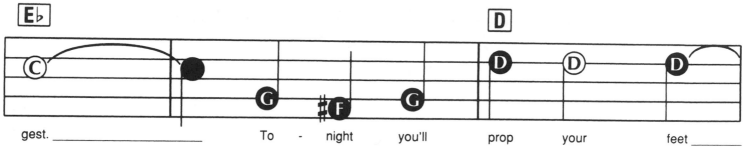

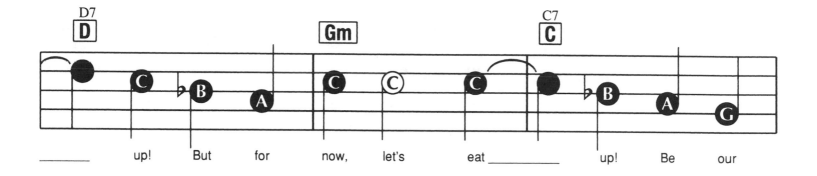

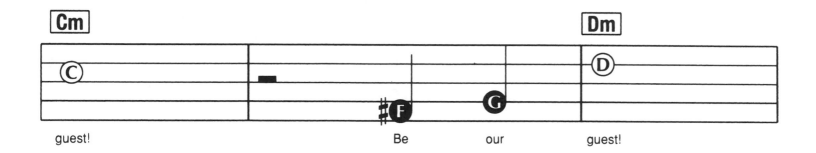

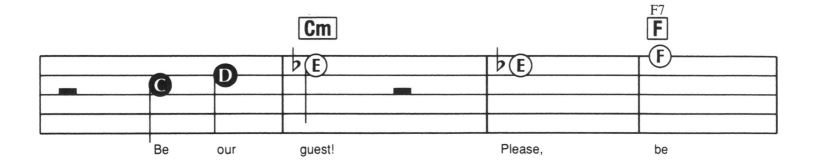

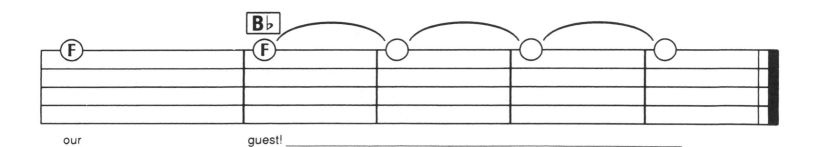

Bibbidi-Bobbidi-Boo
(The Magic Song)
from CINDERELLA

Registration 8
Rhythm: Swing

Words by Jerry Livingston
Music by Mack David and Al Hoffman

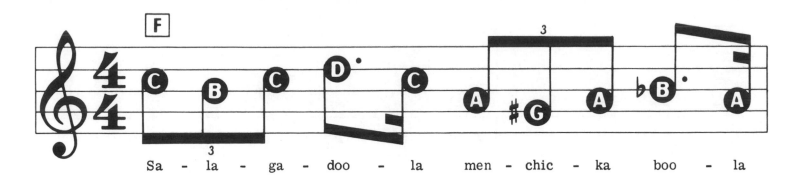

Sa - la - ga - doo - la men - chic - ka boo - la

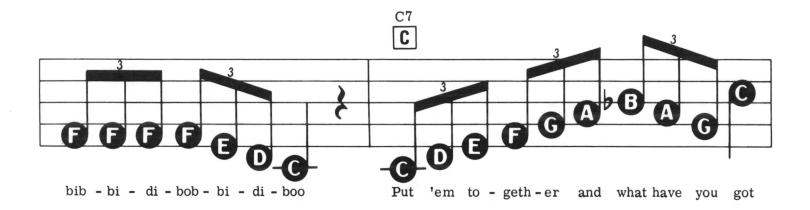

bib - bi - di - bob - bi - di - boo   Put 'em to - geth - er and what have you got

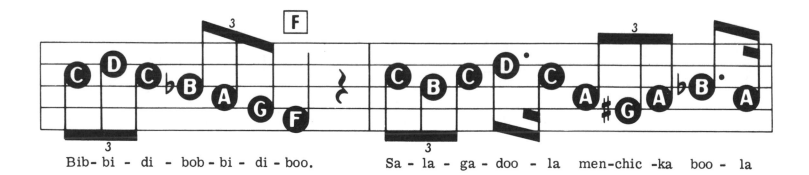

Bib - bi - di - bob - bi - di - boo.   Sa - la - ga - doo - la men - chic - ka boo - la

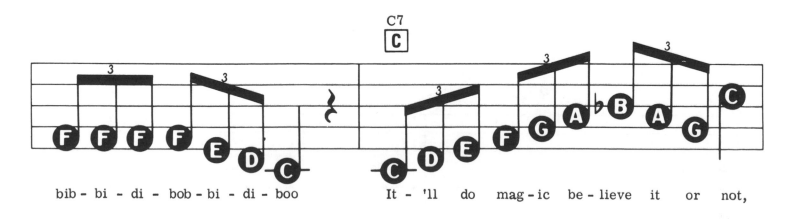

bib - bi - di - bob - bi - di - boo   It - 'll do mag - ic be - lieve it or not,

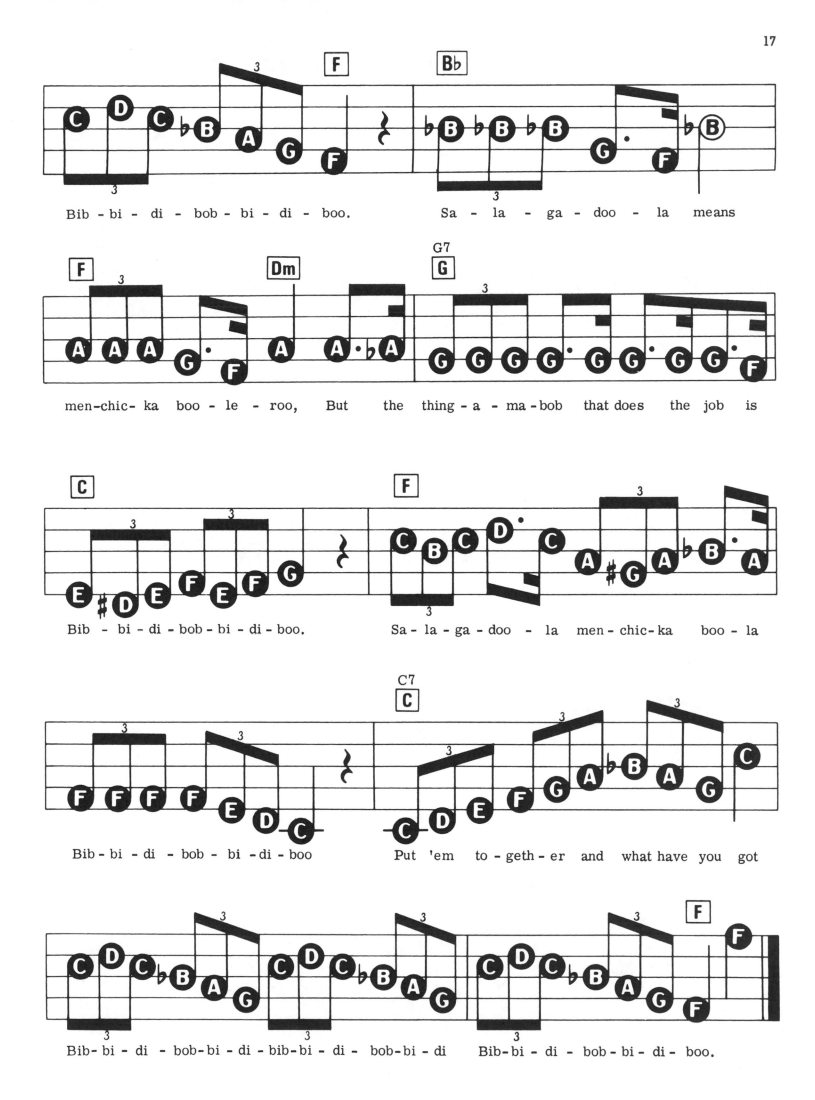

Ev'rybody Wants to Be a Cat
from THE ARISTOCATS

Registration 10
Rhythm: Fox Trot

Words by Floyd Huddleston
Music by Al Rinker

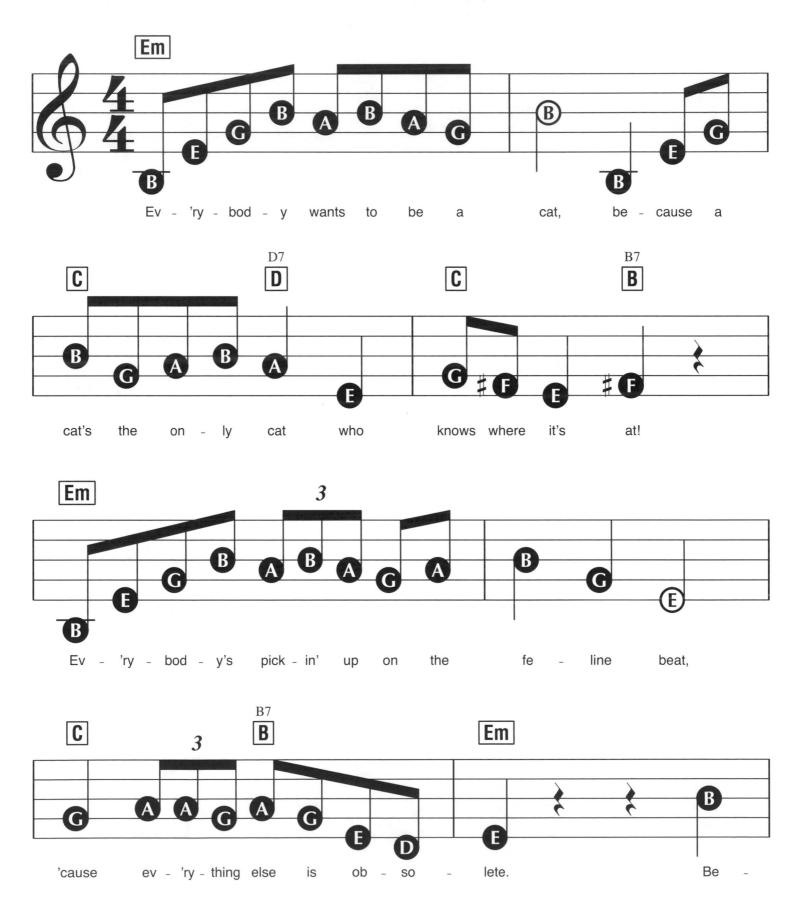

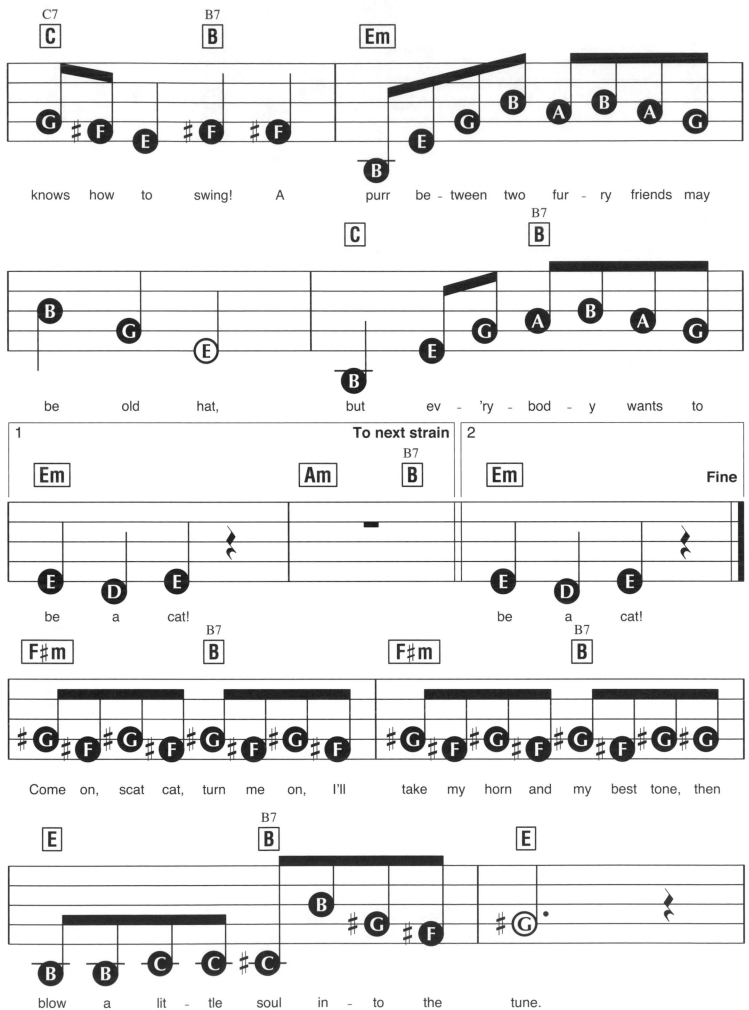

knows how to swing! A purr be – tween two fur – ry friends may

be old hat, but ev – 'ry – bod – y wants to

be a cat!

be a cat!

Come on, scat cat, turn me on, I'll take my horn and my best tone, then

blow a lit – tle soul in – to the tune.

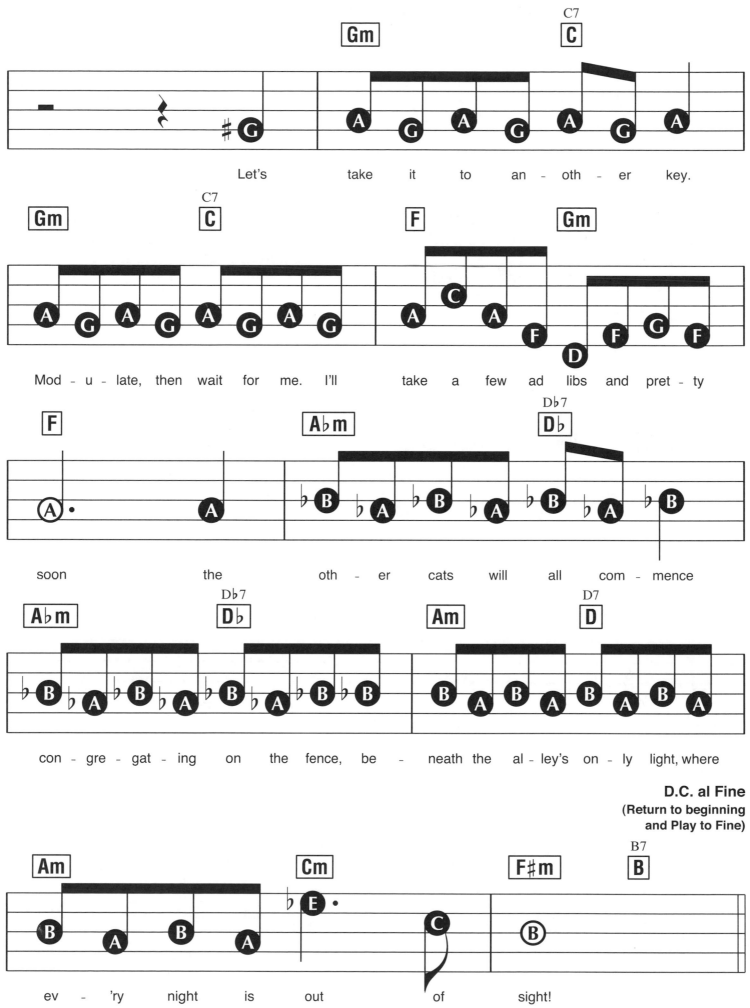

Friend Like Me
from ALADDIN

Registration 1
Rhythm: Polka or March

Music by Alan Menken
Lyrics by Howard Ashman

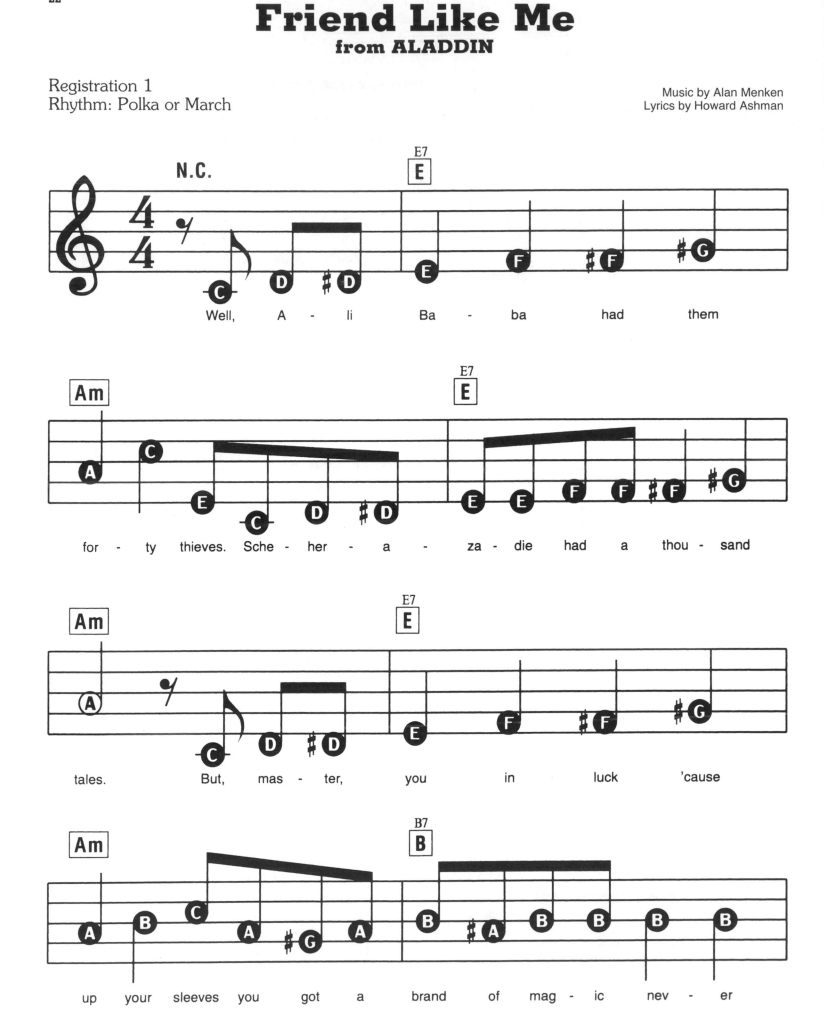

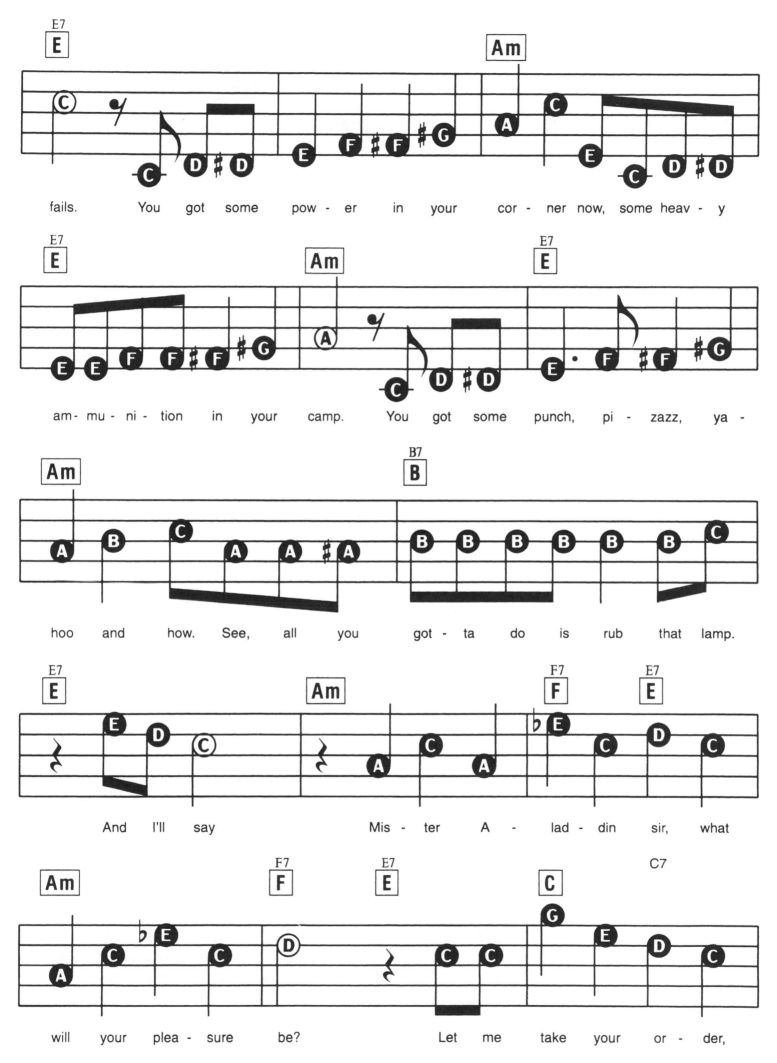

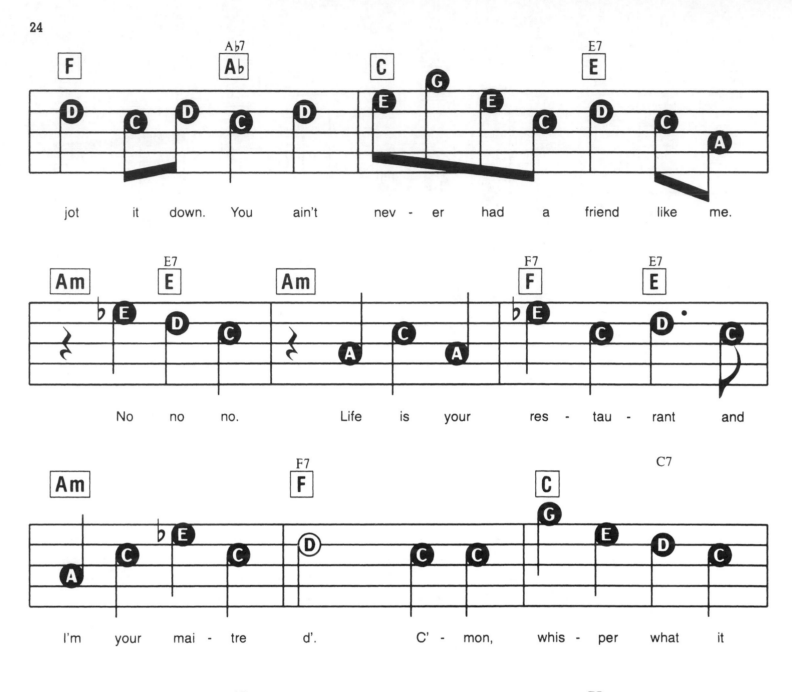

jot it down. You ain't nev - er had a friend like me.

No no no. Life is your res - tau - rant and

I'm your mai - tre d'. C' - mon, whis - per what it

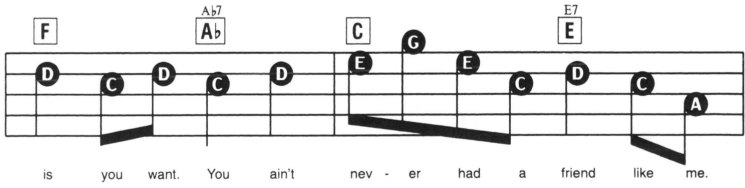

is you want. You ain't nev - er had a friend like me.

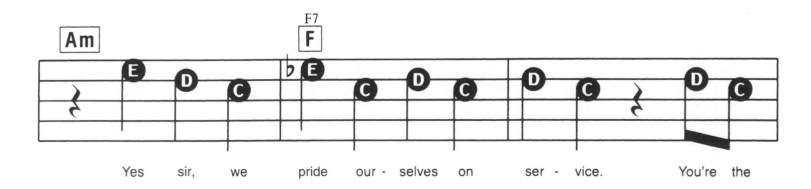

Yes sir, we pride our - selves on ser - vice. You're the

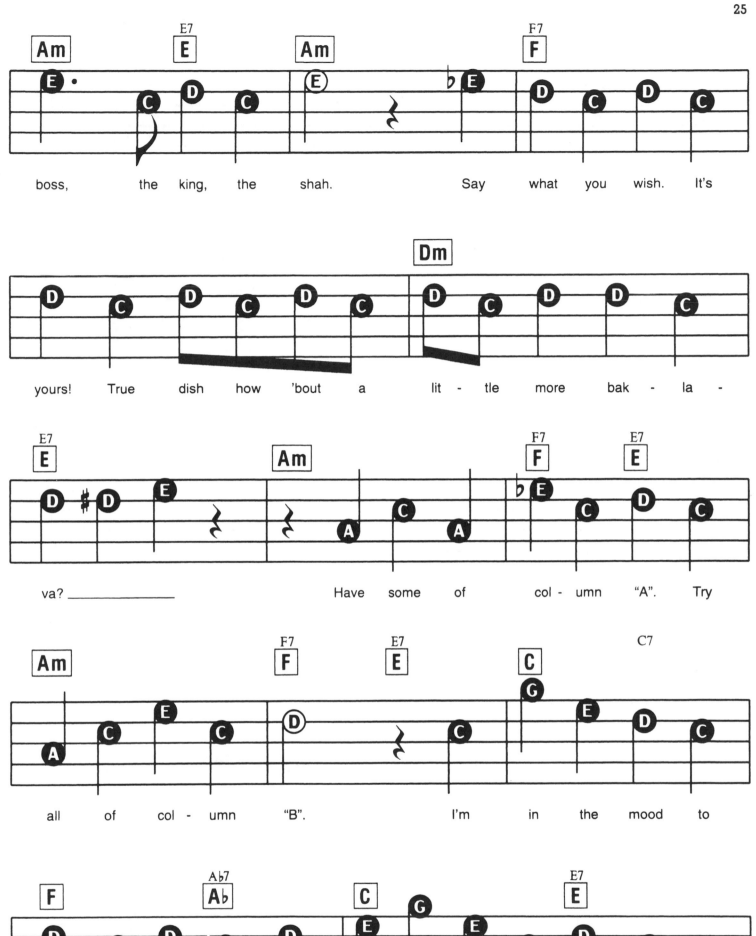

boss, the king, the shah. Say what you wish. It's

yours! True dish how 'bout a lit - tle more bak - la -

va? _____ Have some of col - umn "A". Try

all of col - umn "B". I'm in the mood to

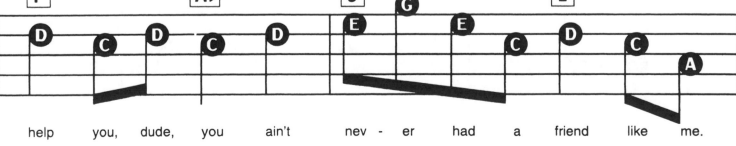

help you, dude, you ain't nev - er had a friend like me.

26

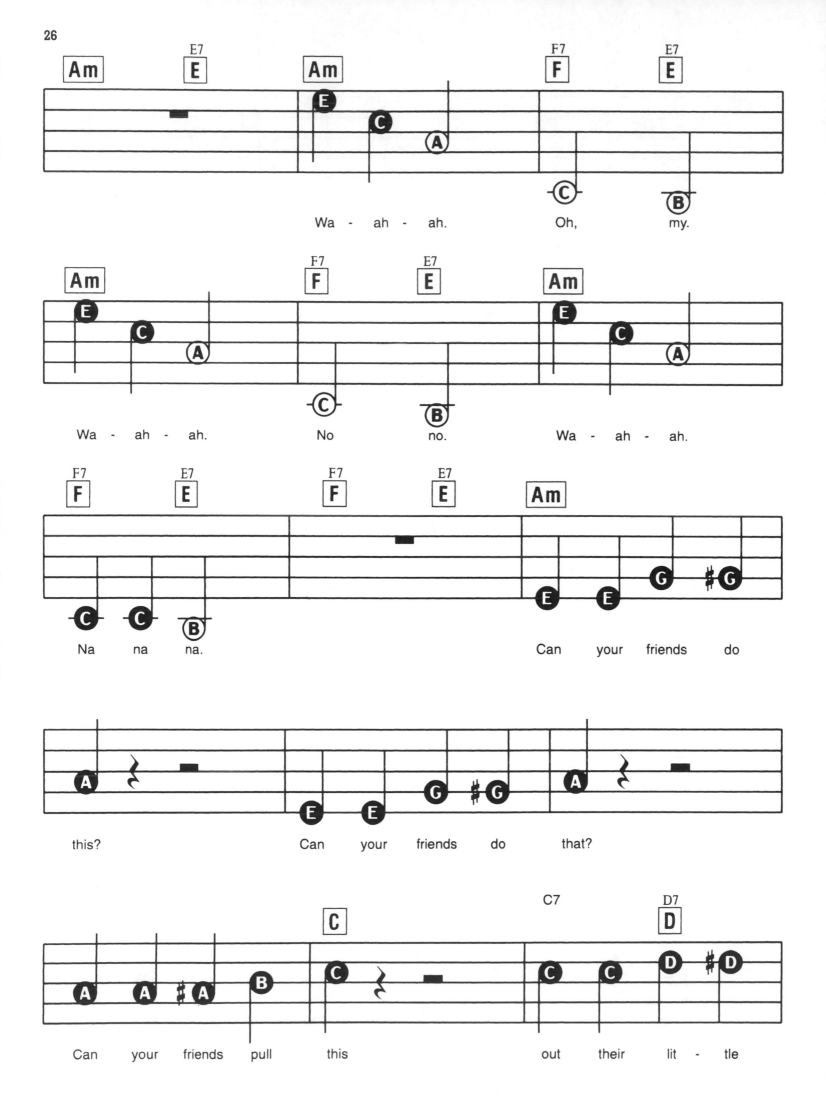

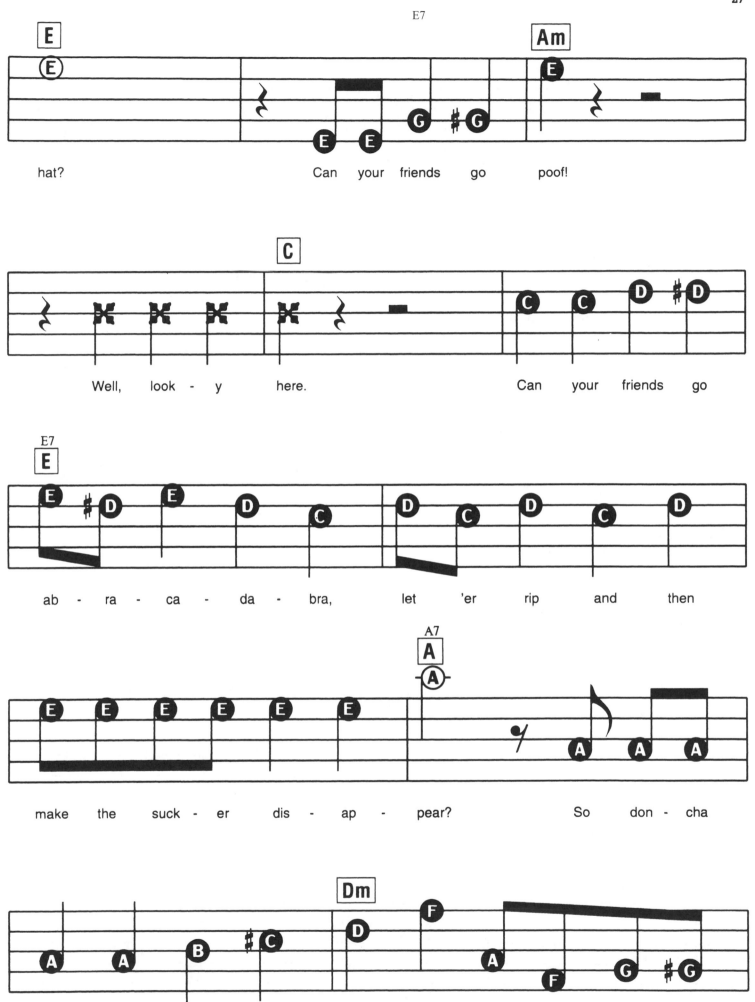

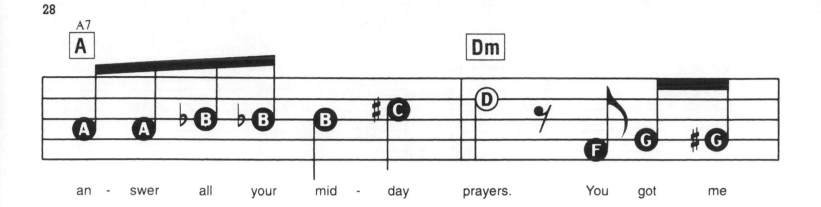

an - swer   all   your   mid - day   prayers.   You   got   me

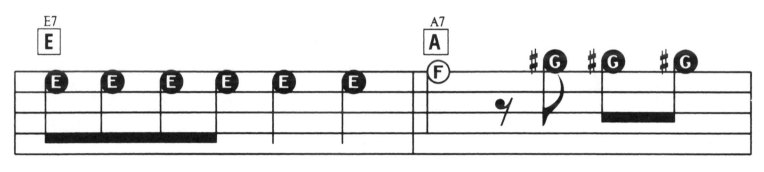

bo - na - fi - de   cer - ti - fied.   You   got   a

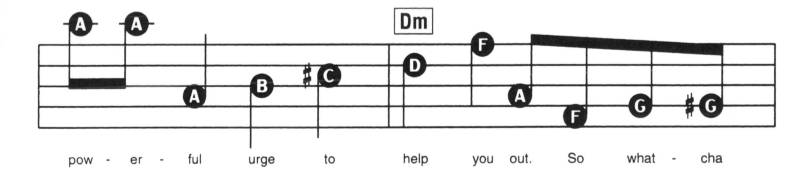

ge - nie   for   your   charge   d'af - faires.   I   got   a

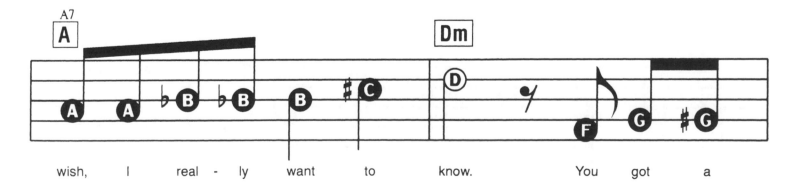

pow - er - ful   urge   to   help   you   out.   So   what - cha

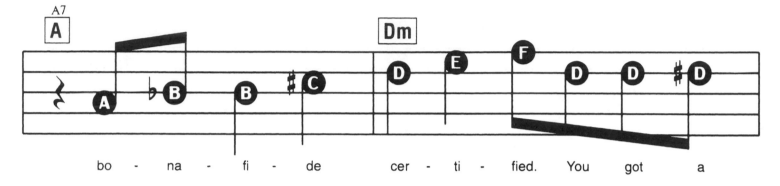

wish,   I   real - ly   want   to   know.   You   got   a

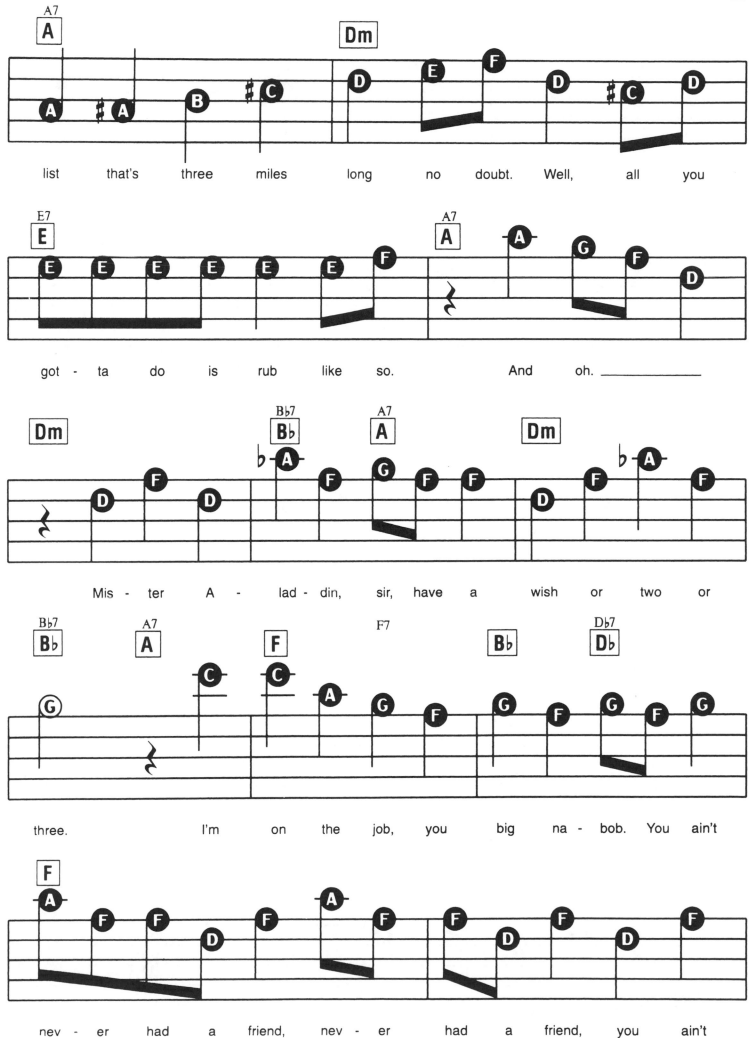

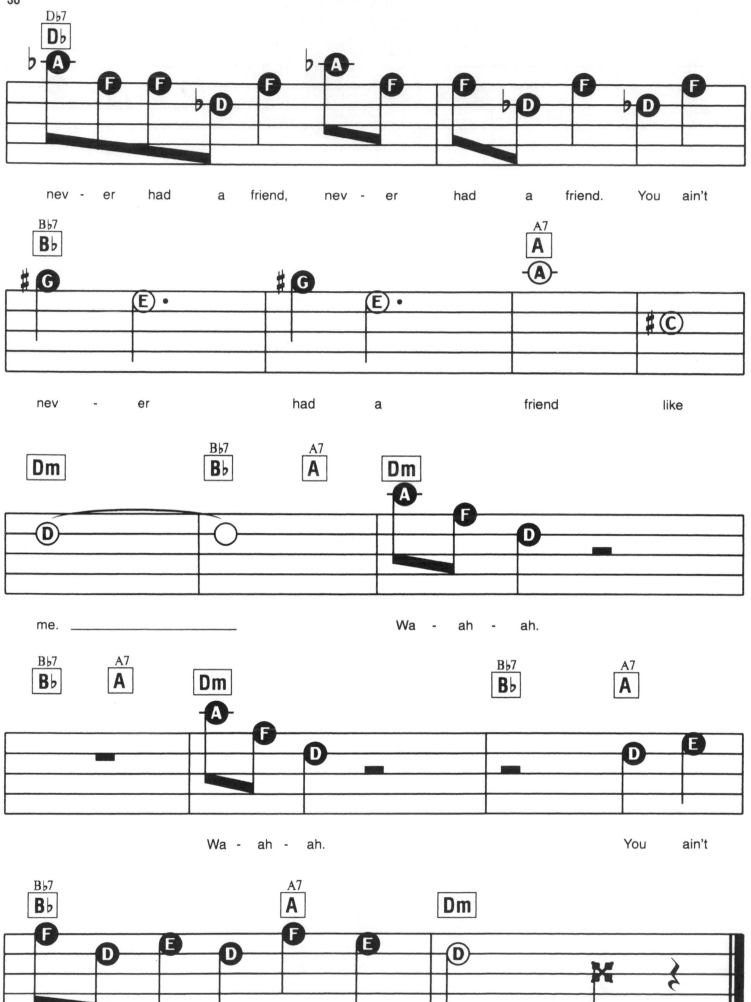

Hakuna Matata
from THE LION KING

Registration 5
Rhythm: Swing

Music by Elton John
Lyrics by Tim Rice

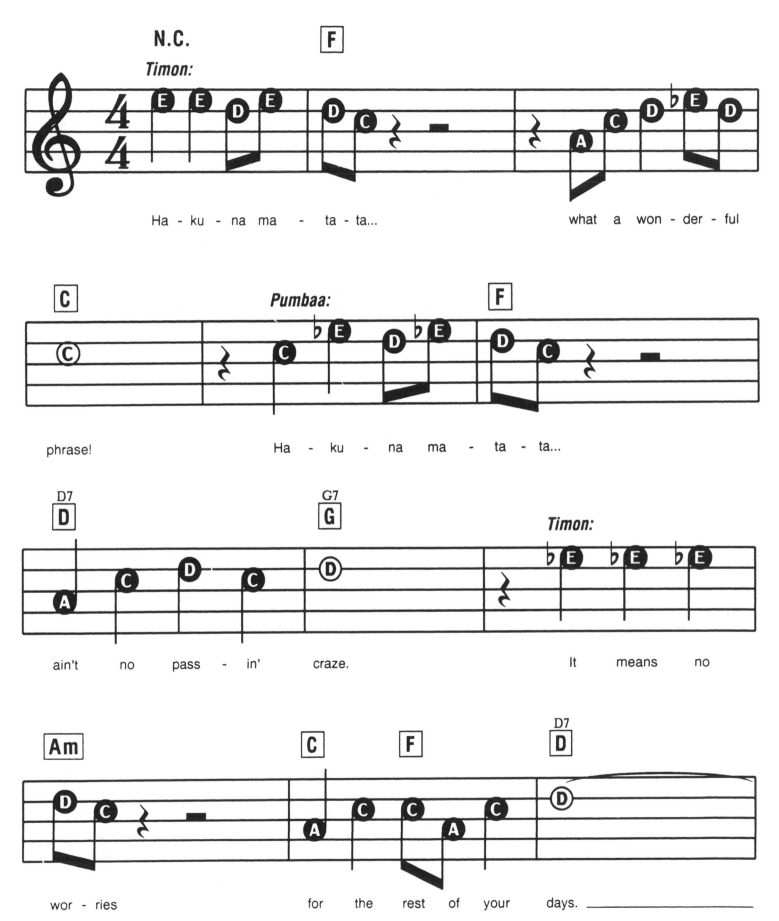

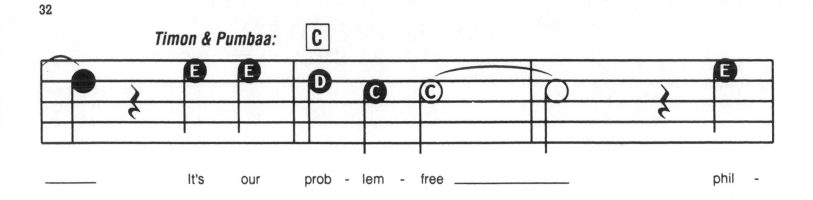

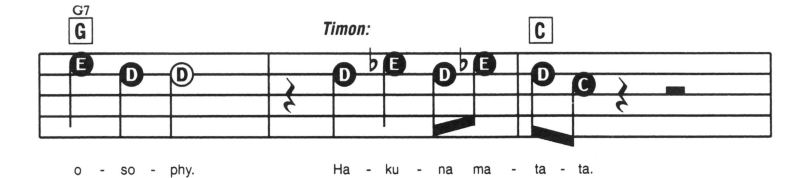

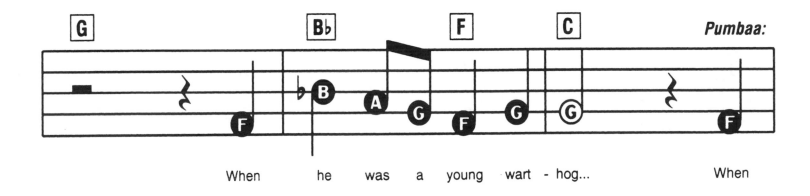

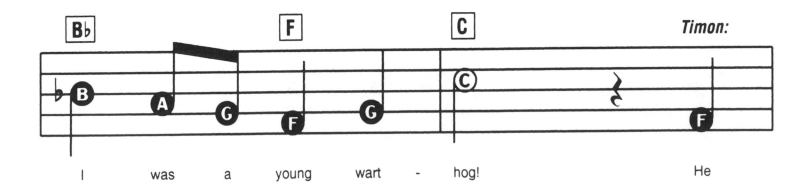

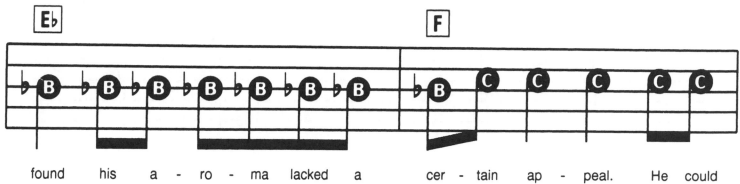

found his a - ro - ma lacked a cer - tain ap - peal. He could

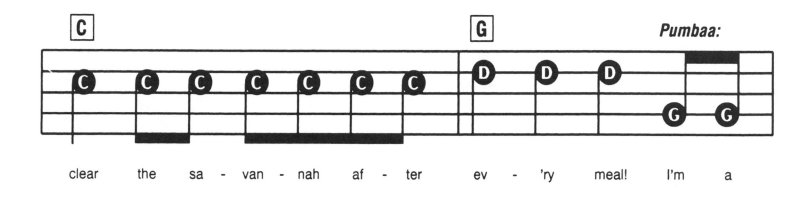

clear the sa - van - nah af - ter ev - 'ry meal! I'm a

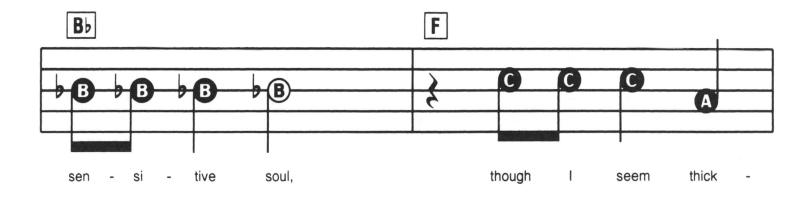

sen - si - tive soul, though I seem thick -

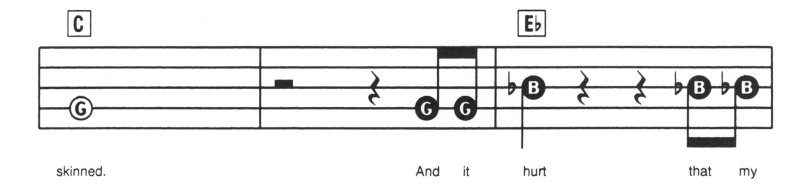

skinned. And it hurt that my

Give a Little Whistle

from PINOCCHIO

Registration 9
Rhythm: Fox Trot or Swing

Words by Ned Washington
Music by Leigh Harline

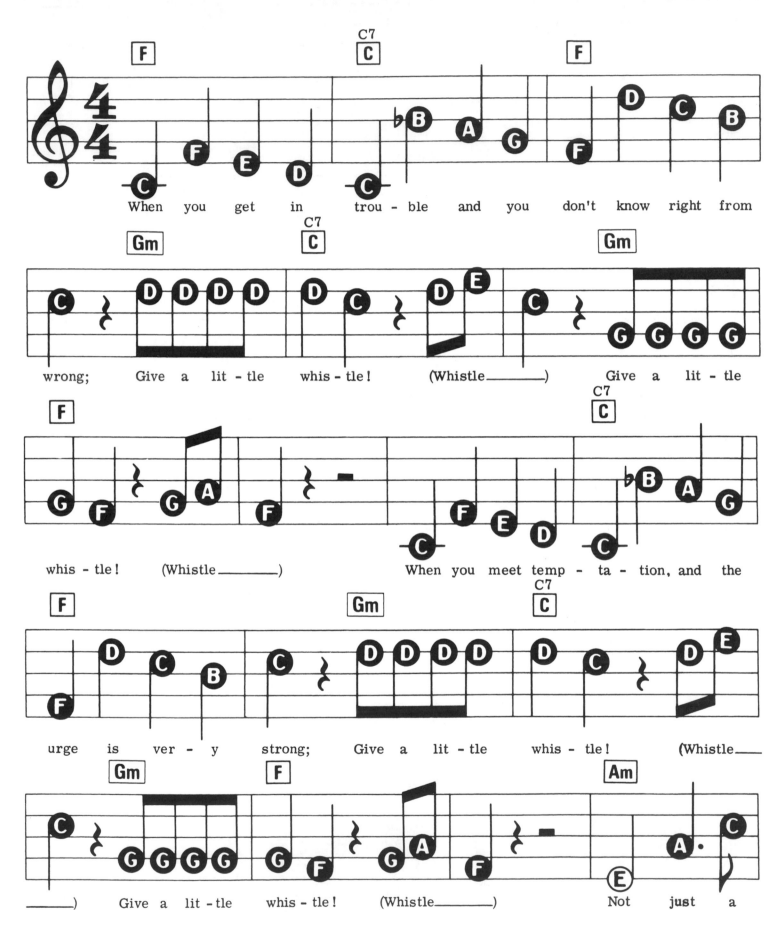

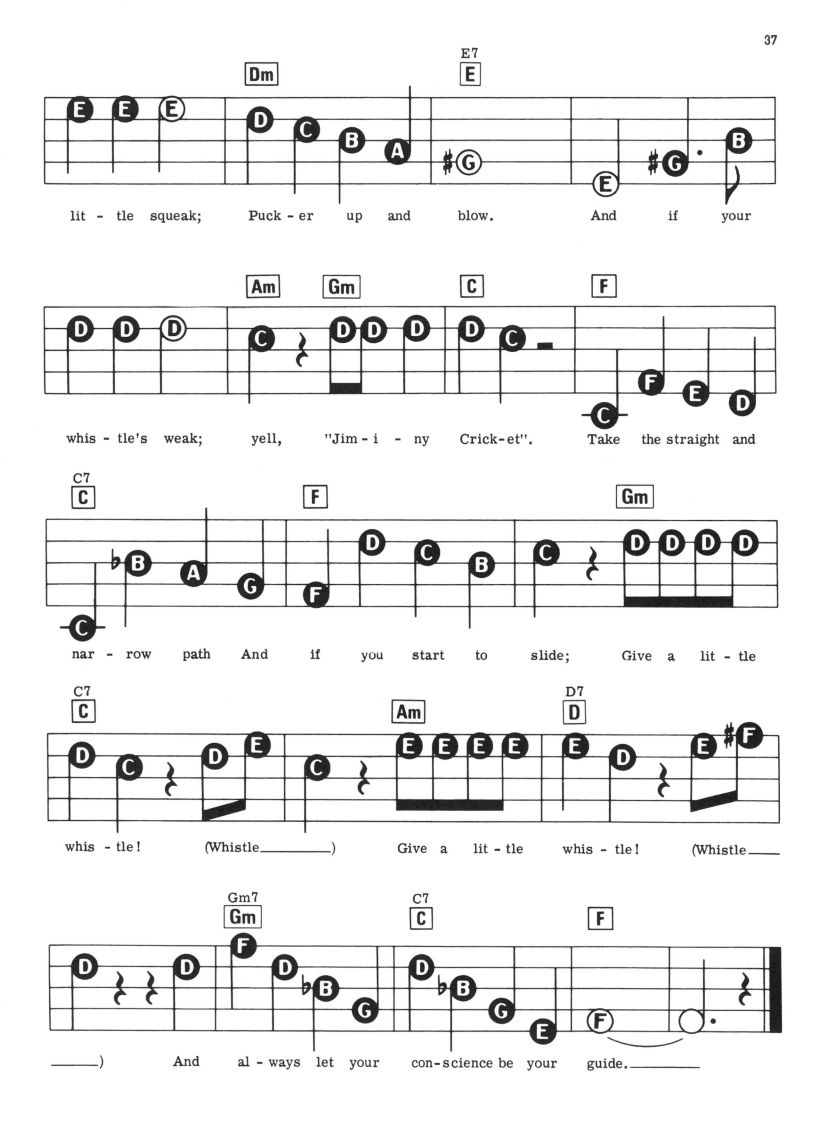

Hawaiian Roller Coaster Ride
from LILO & STITCH

Registration 2
Rhythm: None

Words and Music by Alan Silvestri
and Mark Keali'i Ho'omalu

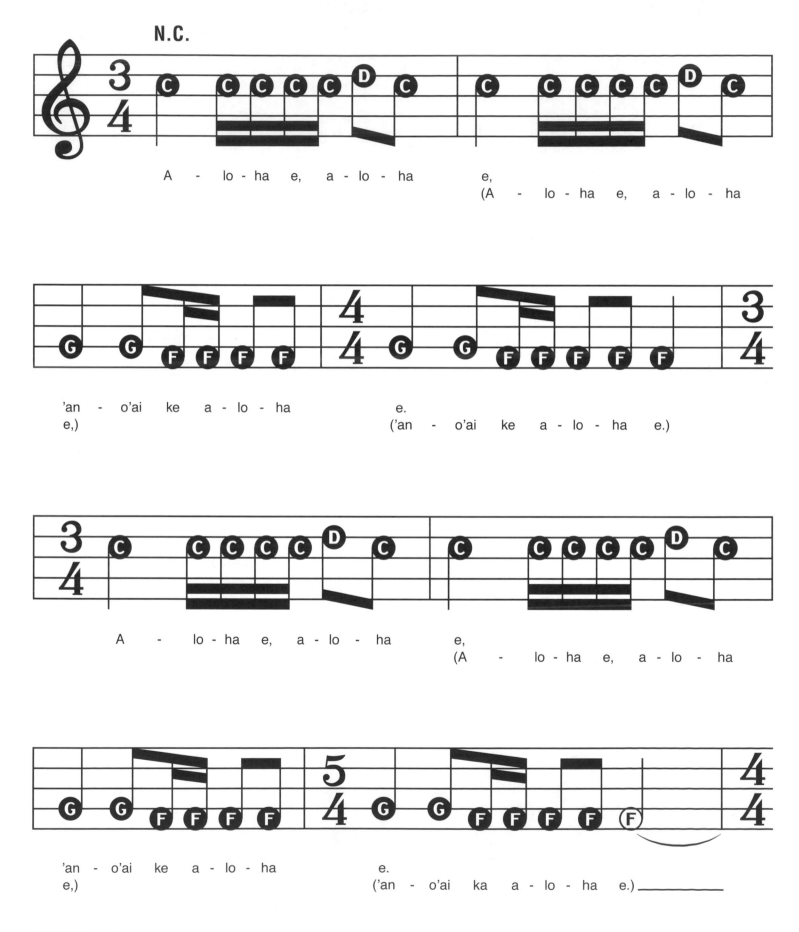

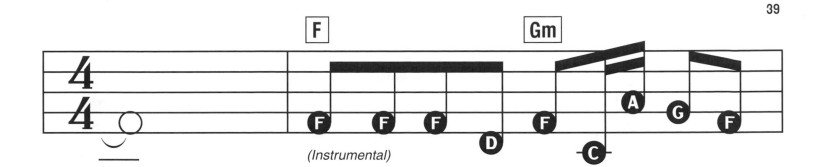

(Instrumental)

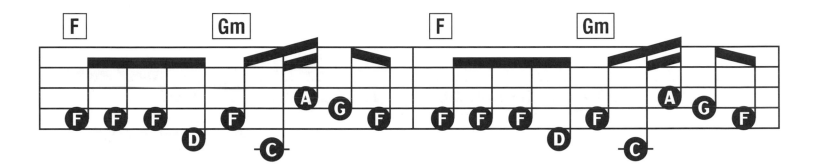

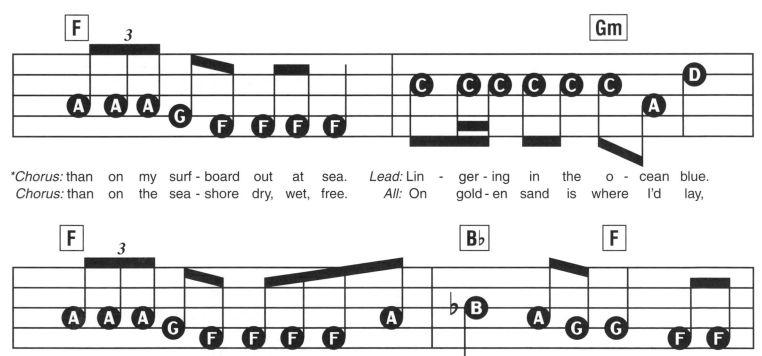

Lead: (1., 3.) There's no place I'd rath - er be
All: (2.) There's no place I'd rath - er be

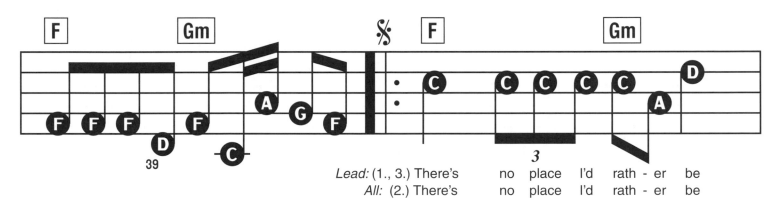

*Chorus: than on my surf - board out at sea. Lead: Lin - ger - ing in the o - cean blue.
Chorus: than on the sea - shore dry, wet, free. All: On gold - en sand is where I'd lay,

Chorus: And if I had one wish come true Lead: I'd surf 'til the sun sets be -
Chorus: and if I on - ly had my way, All: I'd play 'til the sun sets be -

* Childrens' chorus

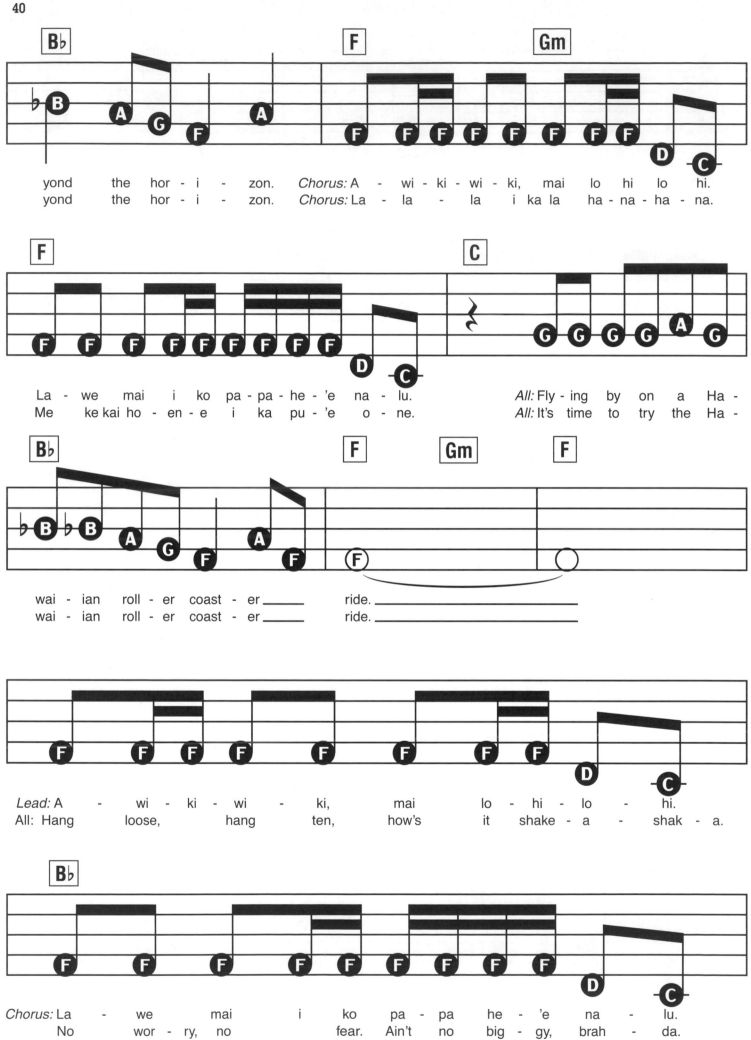

To Coda ⊕

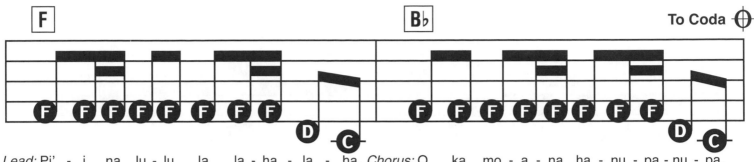

Lead: Pi' - i na lu - lu la la - ha - la - ha. Chorus: O ka mo - a - na ha - nu - pa - nu - pa.
Put - tin' in, cut - tin' up, cut - tin' back, cut - tin' out, Front side, back side, goof - y - foot - ed wipe out.

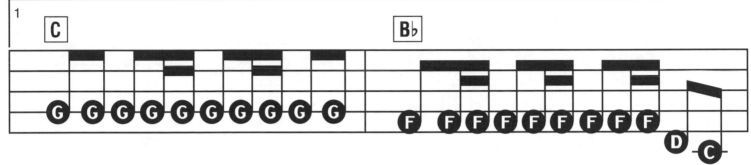

Lead: La - la - la i ka la ha - na - ha - na. Chorus: Me ke kai ho - en - e i ka pu - 'e one.

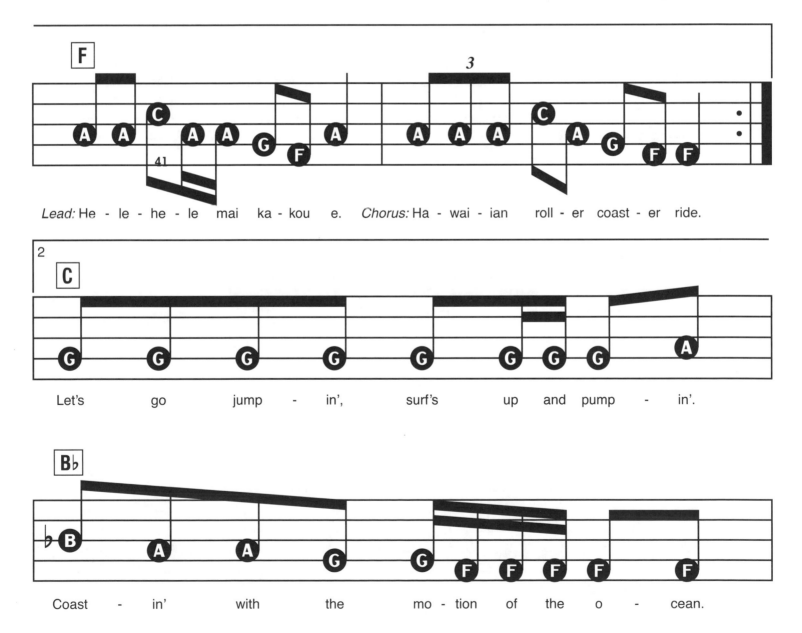

Lead: He - le - he - le mai ka - kou e. Chorus: Ha - wai - ian roll - er coast - er ride.

Let's go jump - in', surf's up and pump - in'.

Coast - in' with the mo - tion of the o - cean.

Un Poco Loco
from COCO

Registration 3
Rhythm: Waltz

Music by Germaine Franco
Lyrics by Adrian Molina

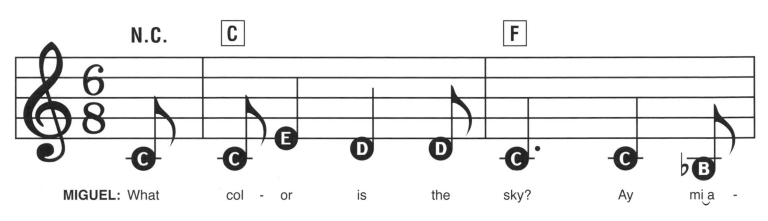

MIGUEL: What col - or is the sky? Ay mi a -

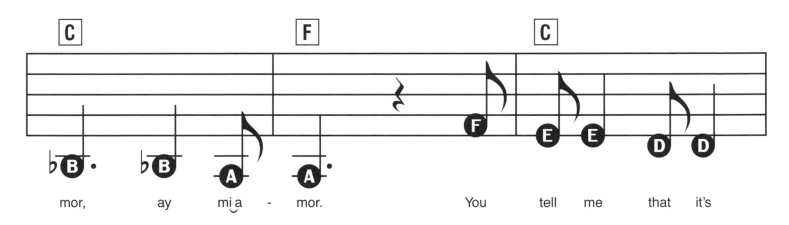

mor, ay mi a - mor. You tell me that it's

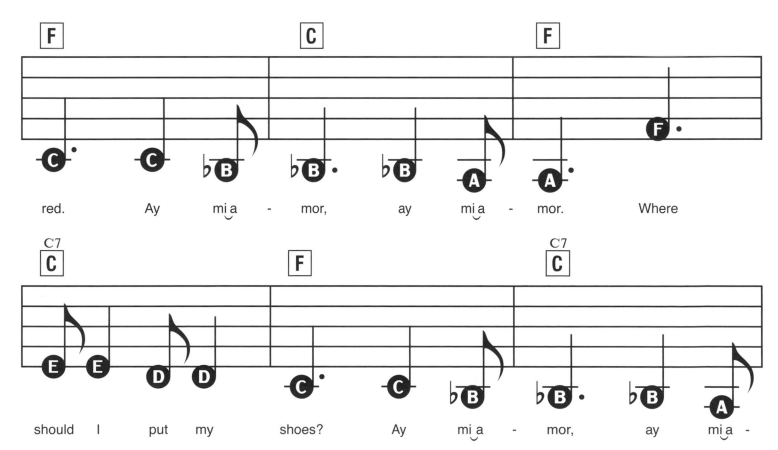

red. Ay mi a - mor, ay mi a - mor. Where

should I put my shoes? Ay mi a - mor, ay mi a -

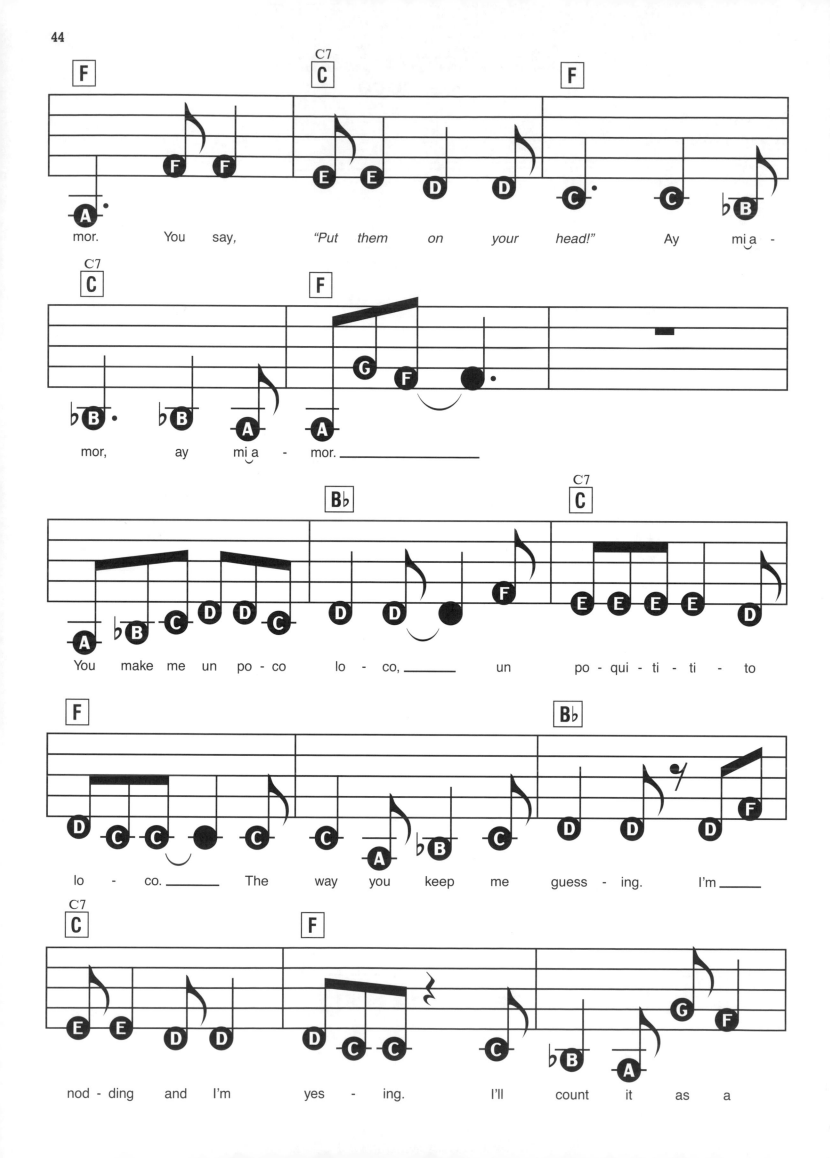

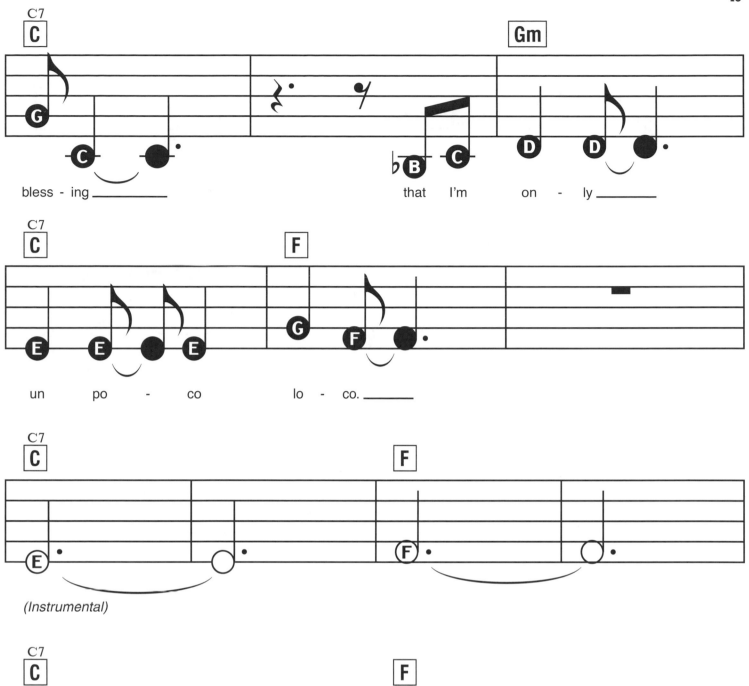

bless - ing _____ that I'm on - ly _____

un po - co lo - co. _____

(Instrumental)

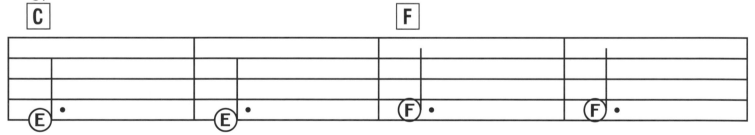

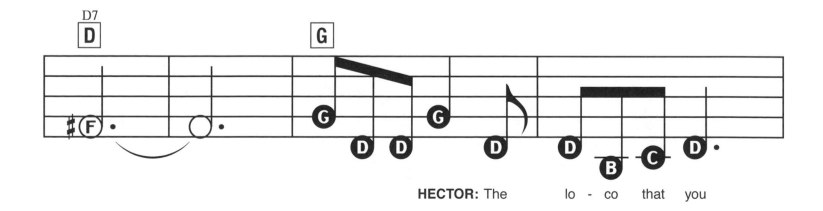

HECTOR: The lo - co that you

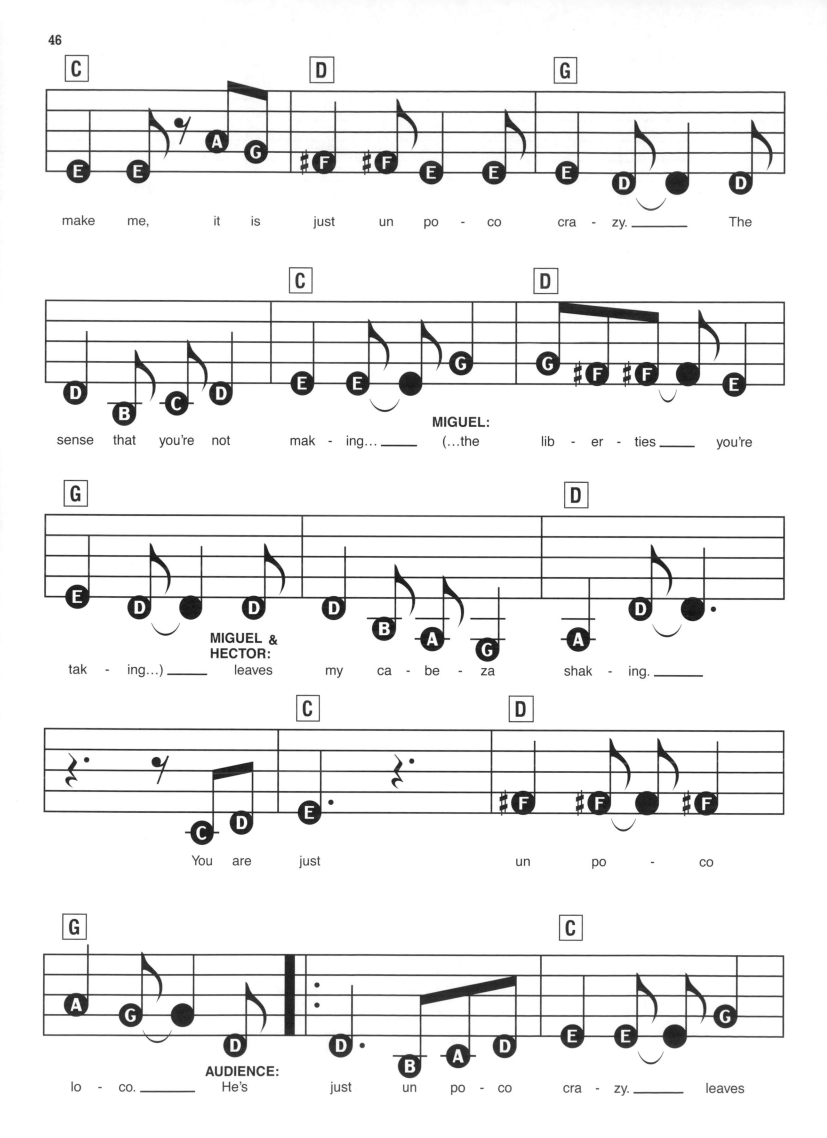

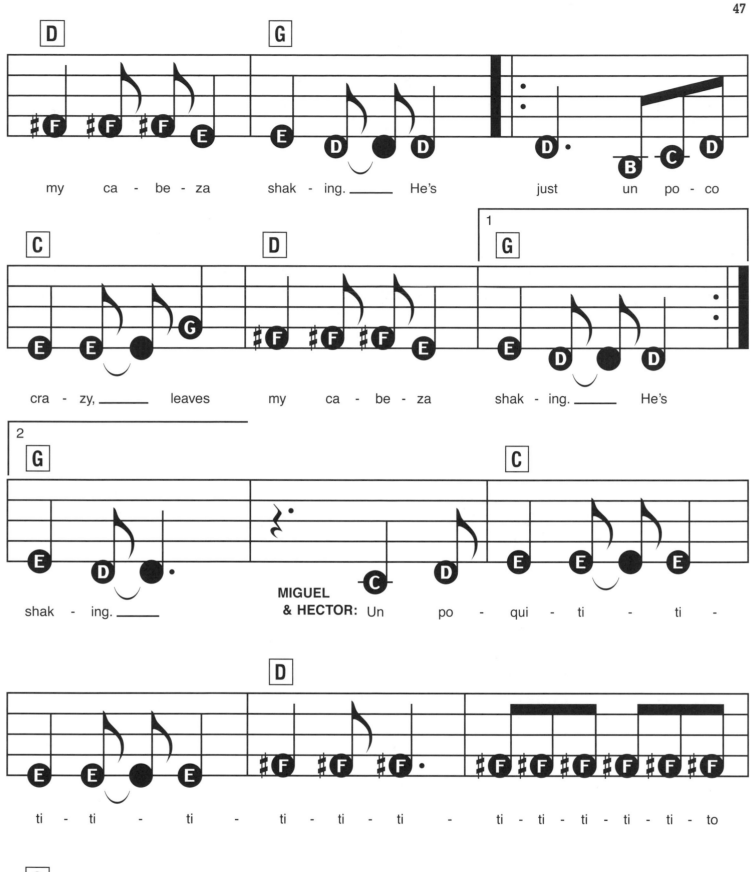

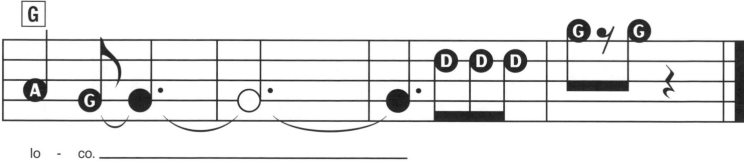

Heigh-Ho
The Dwarfs' Marching Song from
SNOW WHITE AND THE SEVEN DWARFS

Registration 4
Rhythm: March

Words by Larry Morey
Music by Frank Churchill

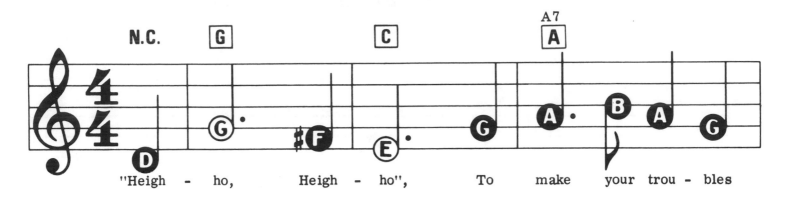

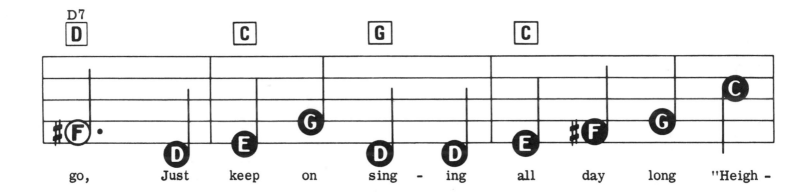

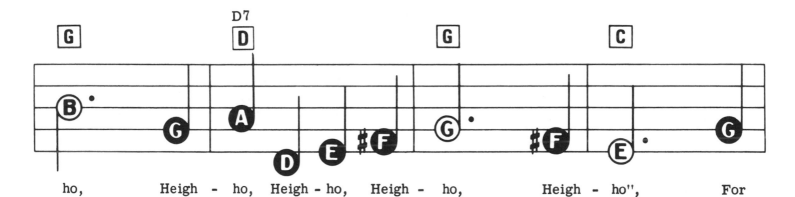

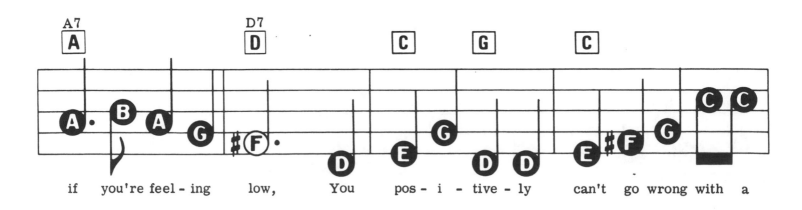

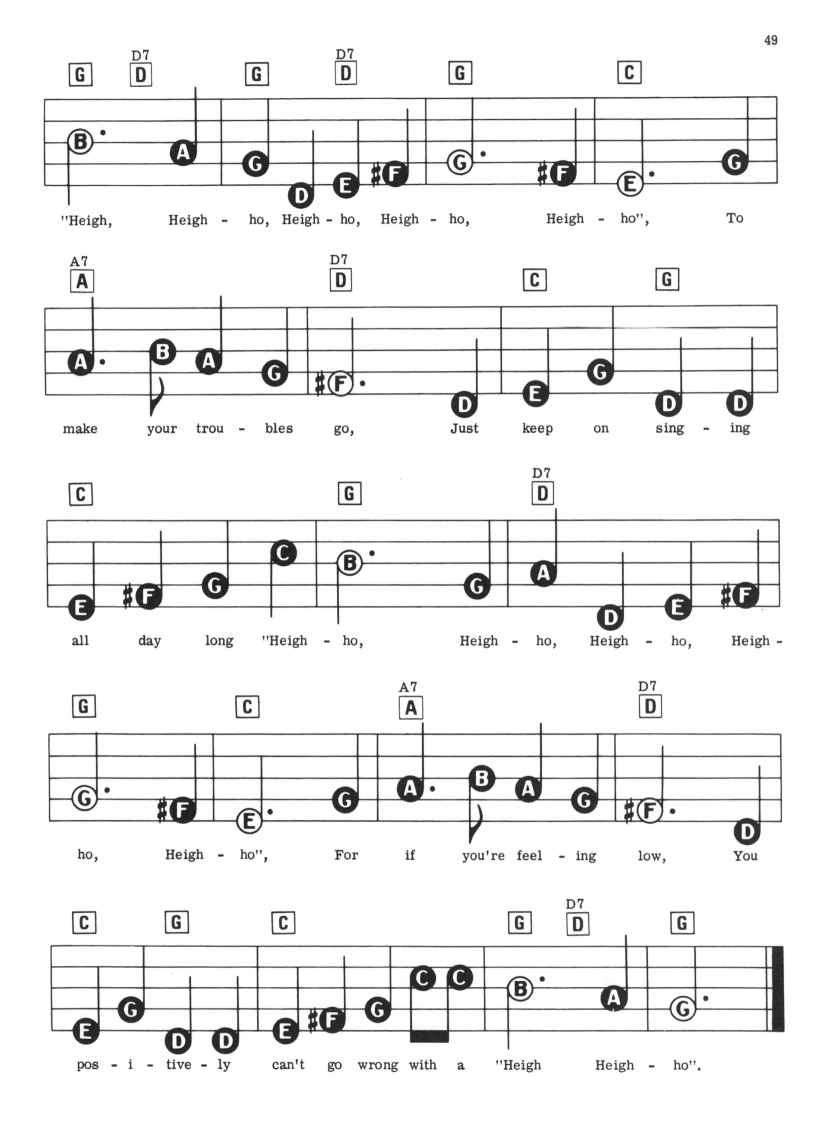

I Just Can't Wait to Be King

from THE LION KING

Registration 8
Rhythm: Motown or Rock

Music by Elton John
Lyrics by Tim Rice

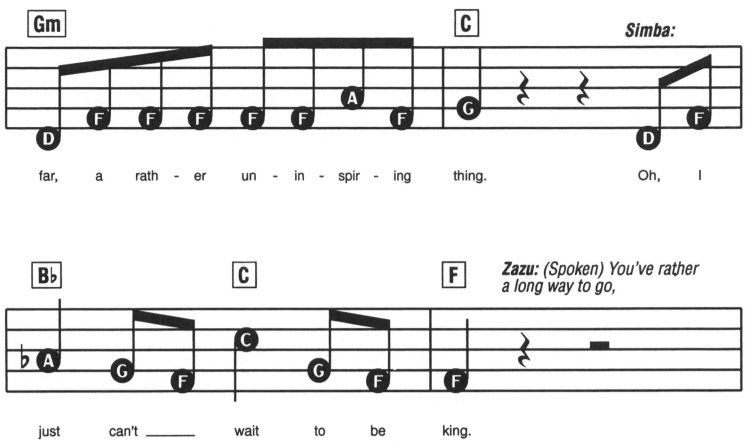

Gm
C
Simba:
far, a rath - er un - in - spir - ing thing. Oh, I
Bb
C
F
Zazu: (Spoken) You've rather a long way to go,
just can't wait to be king.
young Master! If you think...
Bb
Now when I said that I...
No one say - ing "do this," no one say - ing
Gm
What I meant was that the...
C
But what you don't realize...
"be there," no one say - ing "stop that," no one say - ing

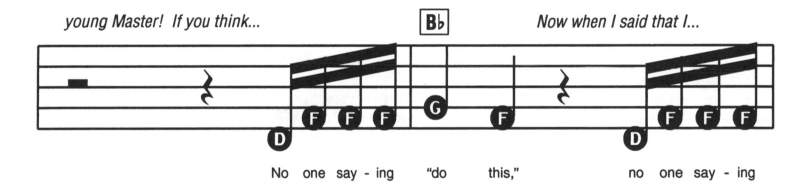

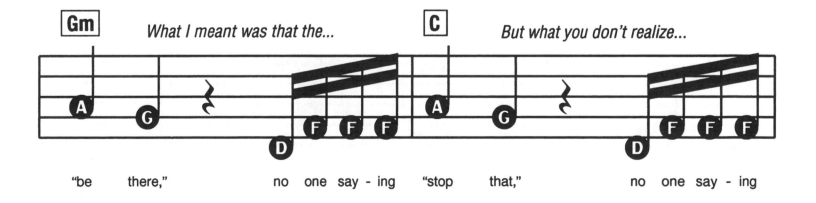

52

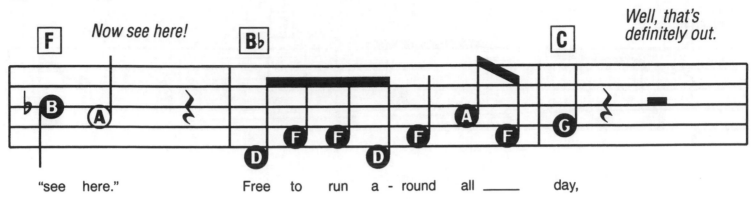

F — *Now see here!*　Bb　C　*Well, that's definitely out.*

"see here."　Free to run a - round all ____ day,

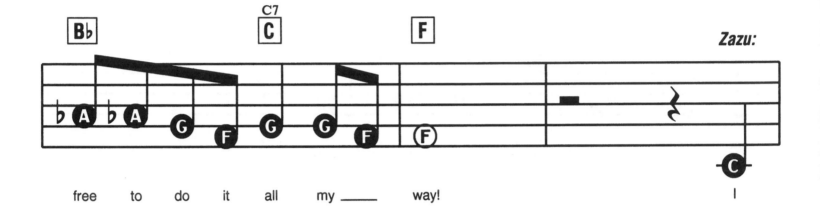

Bb　C7 / C　F　*Zazu:*

free to do it all my ____ way!　I

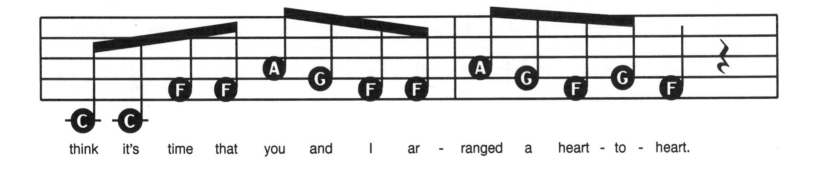

think it's time that you and I ar - ranged a heart - to - heart.

Simba:
Bb　F　*Zazu:*

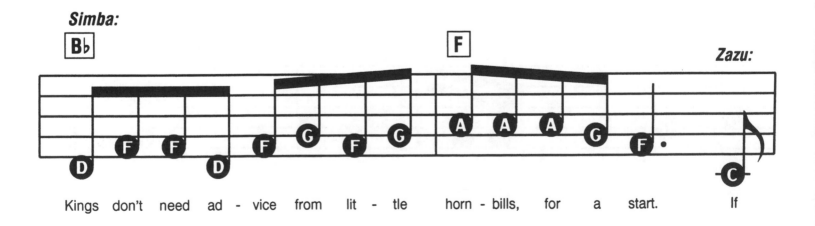

Kings don't need ad - vice from lit - tle horn - bills, for a start.　If

53

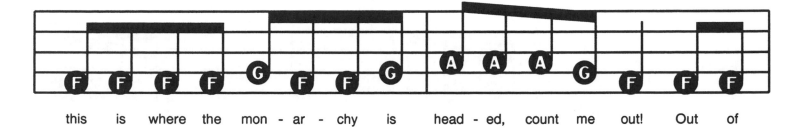

this is where the mon - ar - chy is head - ed, count me out! Out of

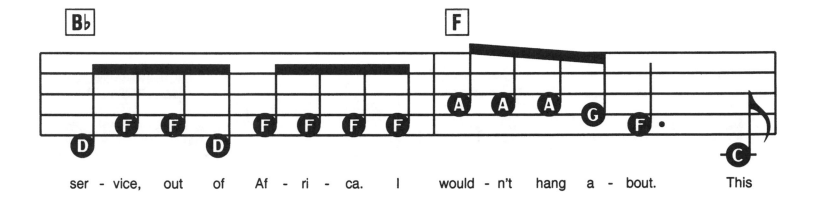

ser - vice, out of Af - ri - ca. I would - n't hang a - bout. This

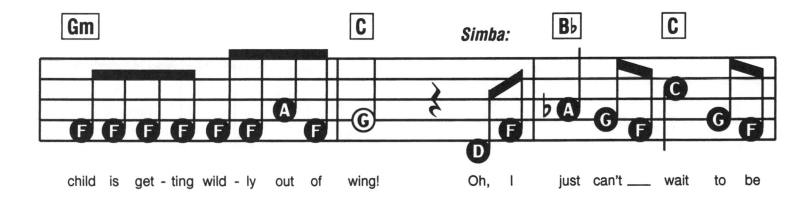

child is get - ting wild - ly out of wing! Oh, I just can't ___ wait to be

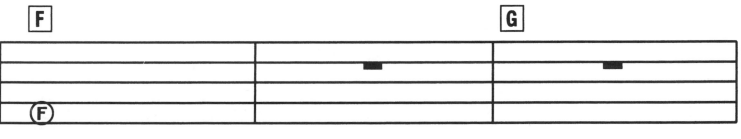

king!

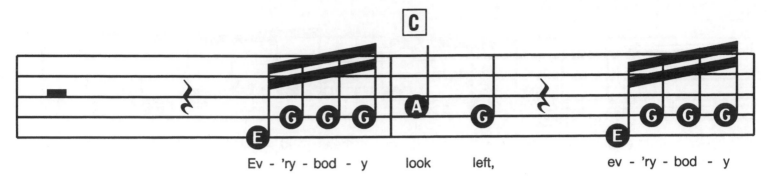

Ev - 'ry - bod - y look left, ev - 'ry - bod - y

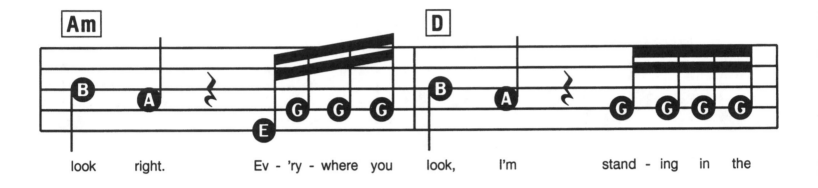

look right. Ev - 'ry - where you look, I'm stand - ing in the

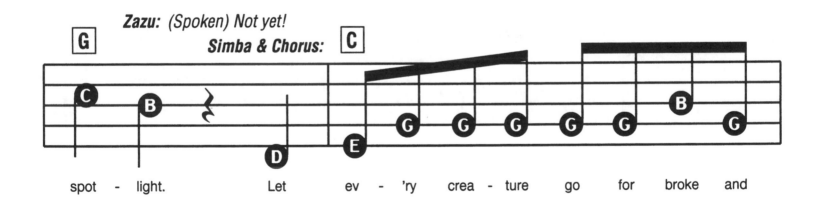

Zazu: *(Spoken) Not yet!*

Simba & Chorus:

spot - light. Let ev - 'ry crea - ture go for broke and

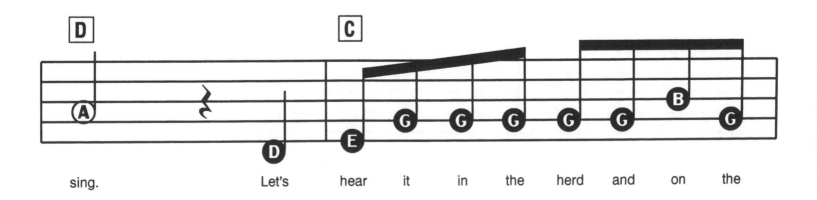

sing. Let's hear it in the herd and on the

I've Got No Strings
from PINOCCHIO

Registration 2
Rhythm: Fox Trot or Swing

Words by Ned Washington
Music by Leigh Harline

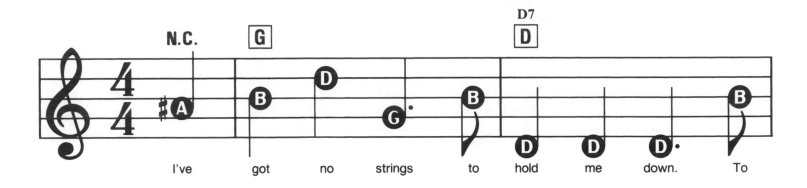

I've got no strings to hold me down. To

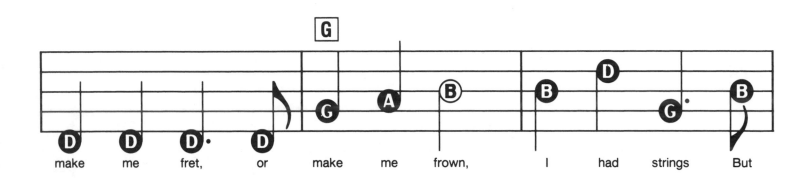

make me fret, or make me frown, I had strings But

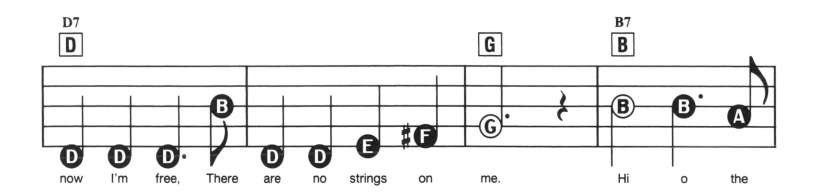

now I'm free, There are no strings on me. Hi o the

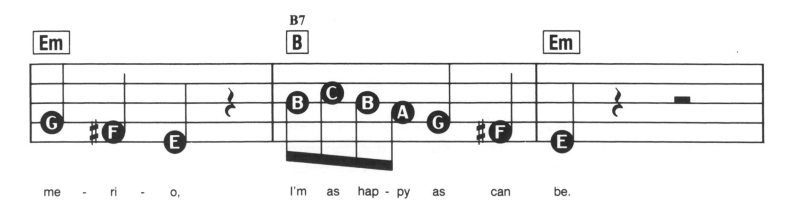

me - ri - o, I'm as hap - py as can be.

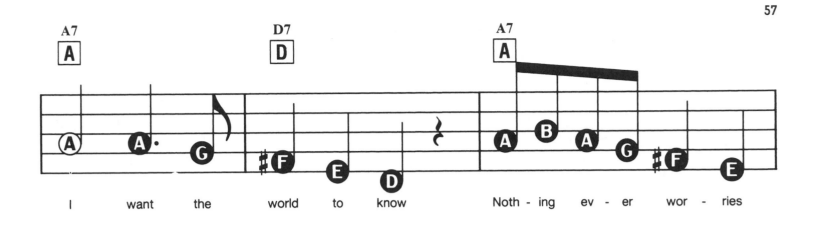

I want the world to know Noth-ing ev-er wor-ries

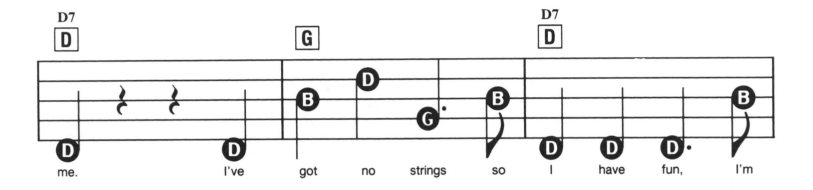

me. I've got no strings so I have fun, I'm

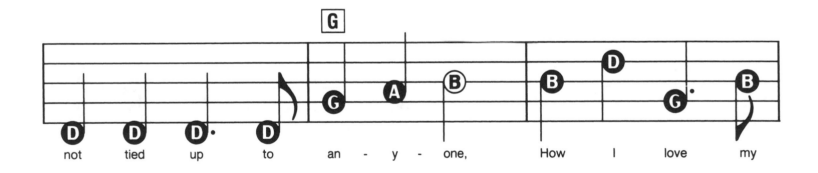

not tied up to an-y-one, How I love my

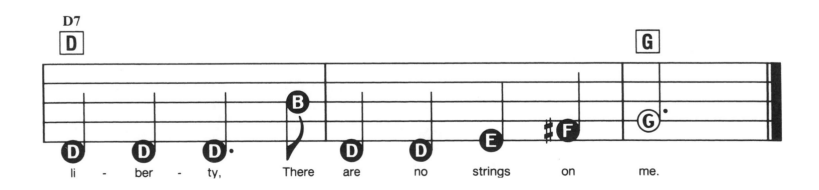

li-ber-ty, There are no strings on me.

If I Didn't Have You
from MONSTERS, INC.

Registration 7
Rhythm: Fox Trot or Swing

Music and Lyrics by
Randy Newman

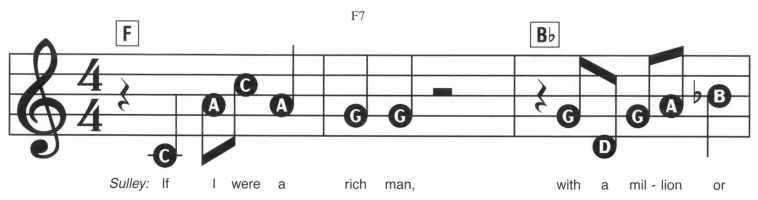

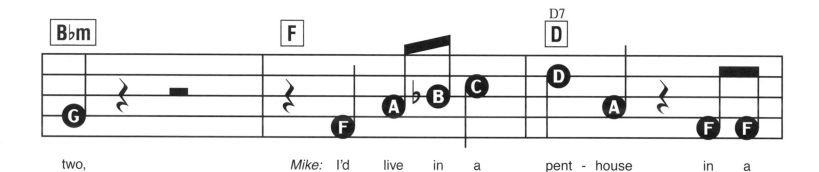

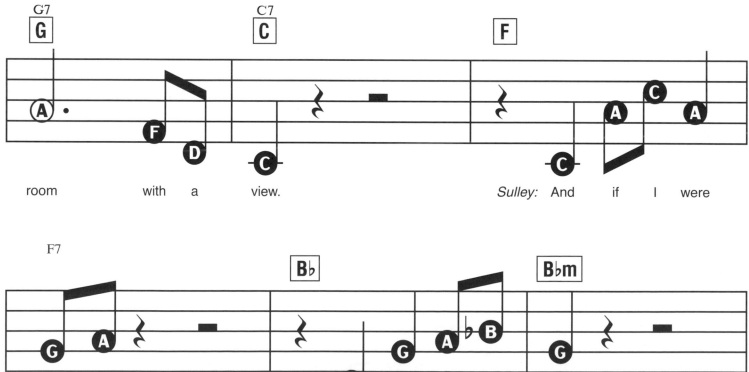

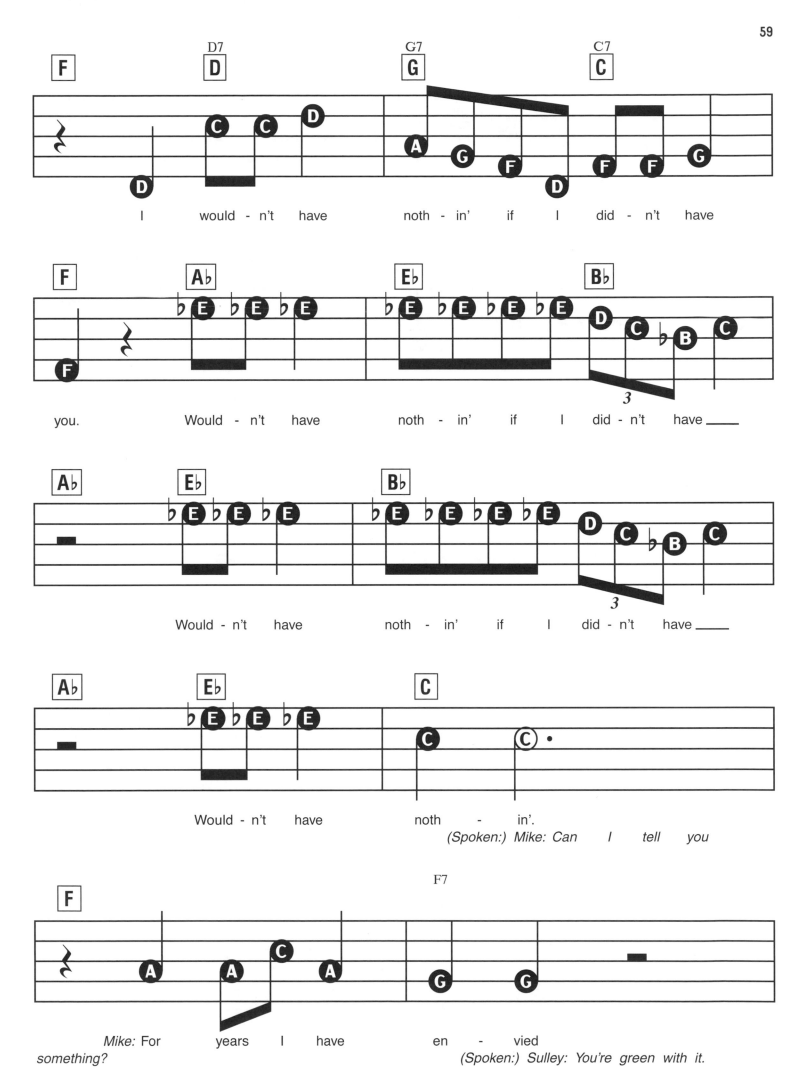

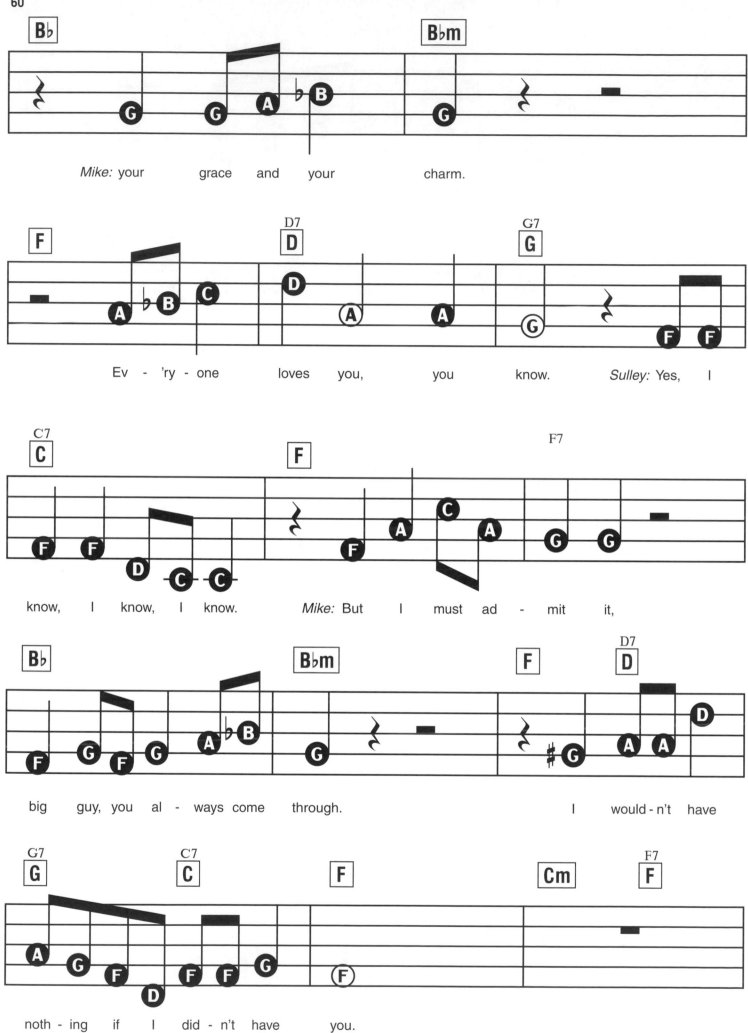

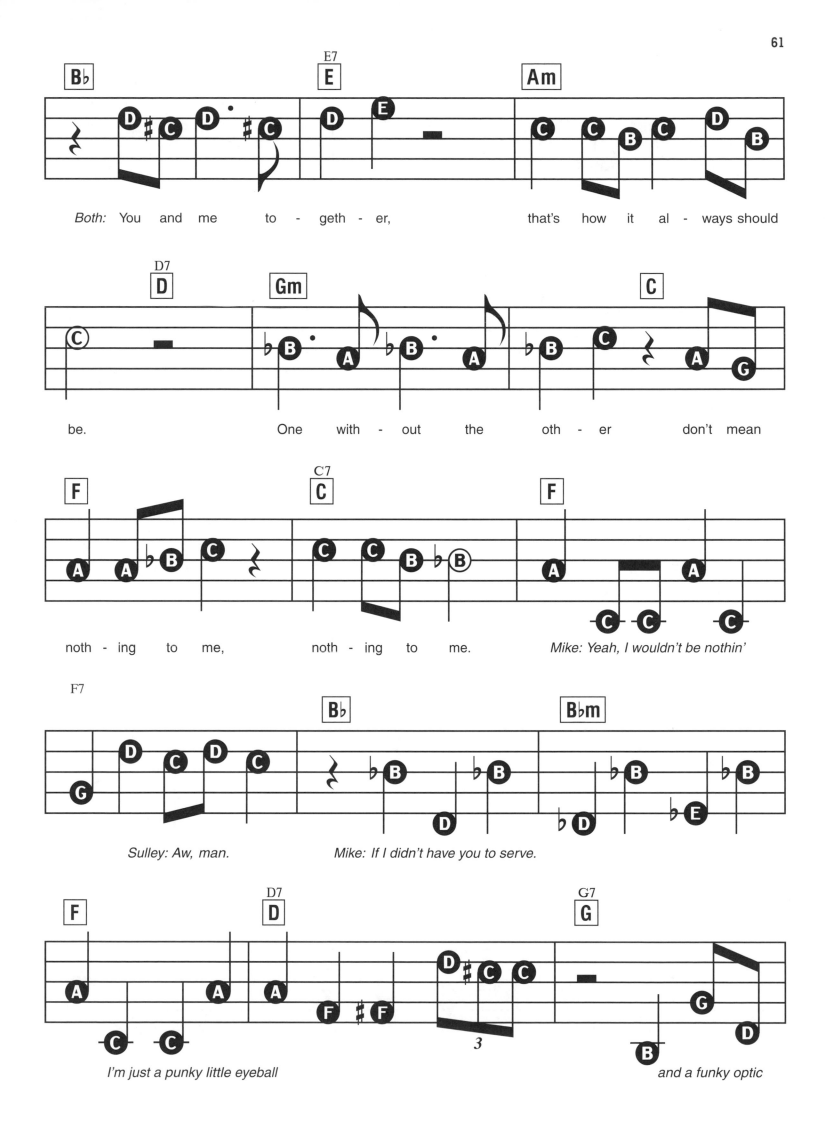

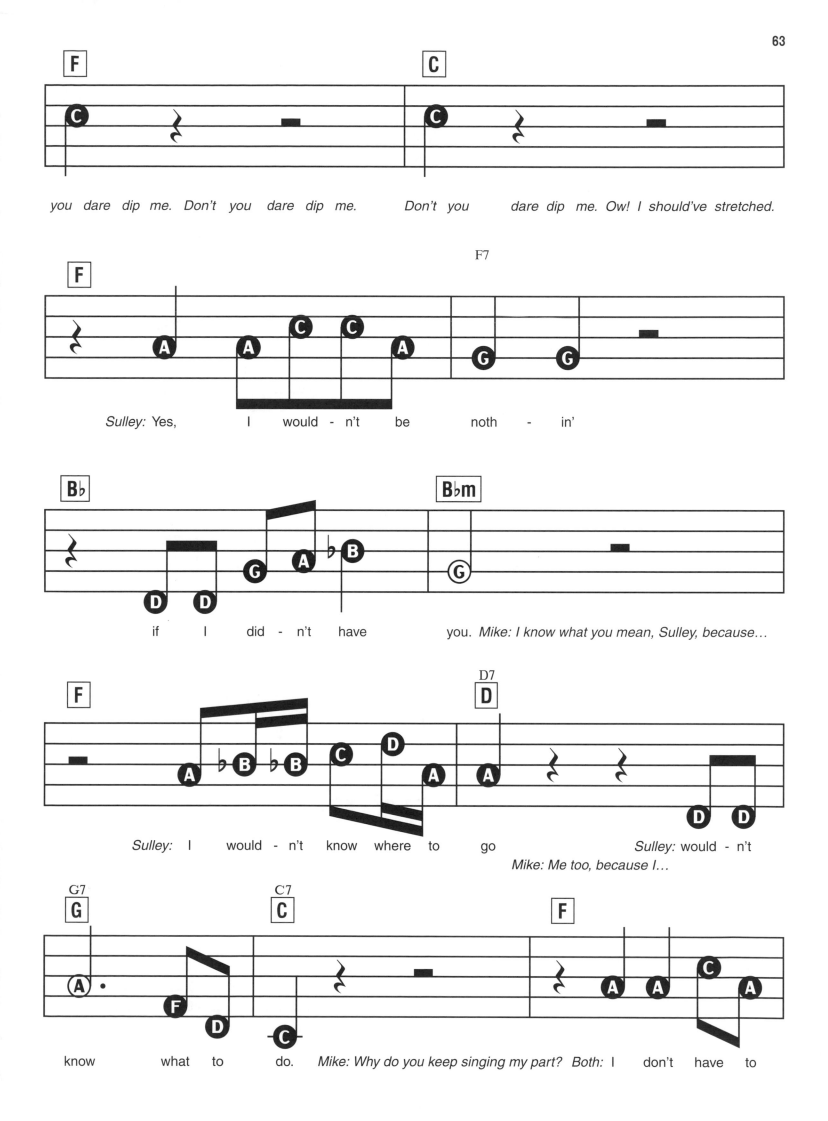

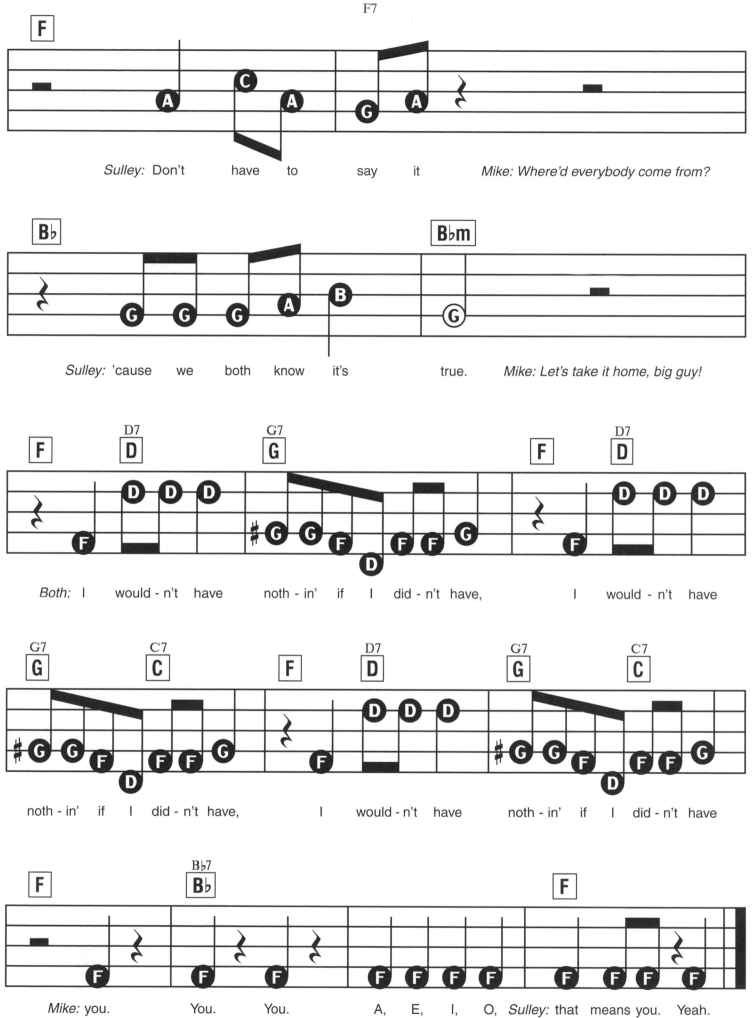

In Summer
from FROZEN

Registration 1
Rhythm: Fox Trot or Swing

Music and Lyrics by Kristen Anderson-Lopez
and Robert Lopez

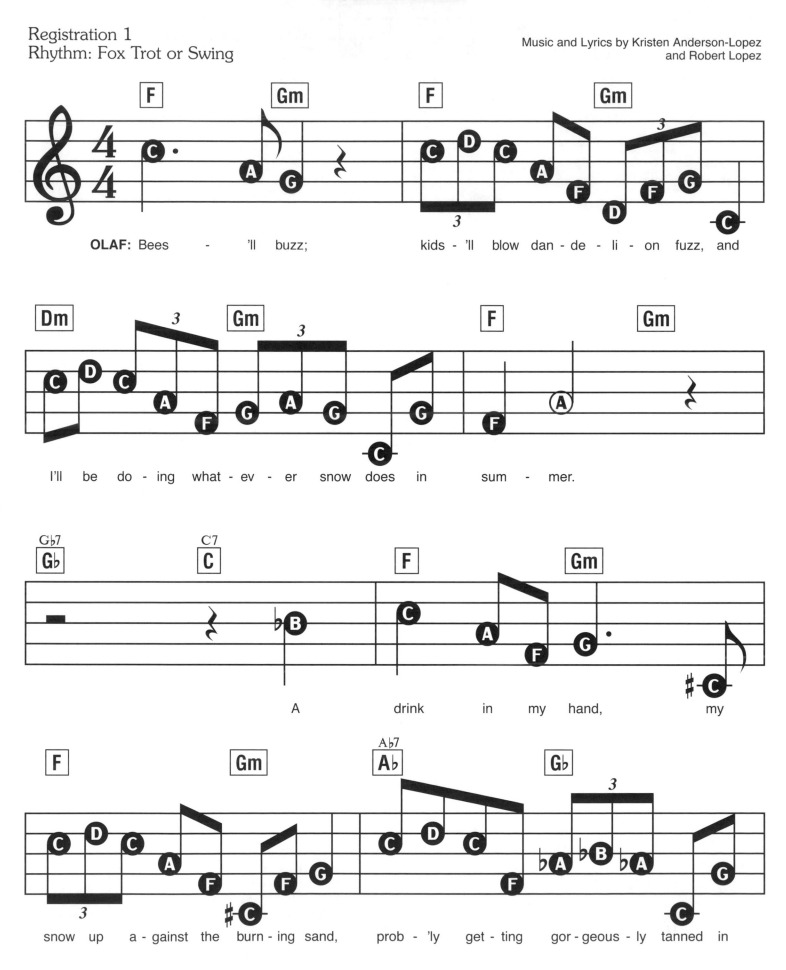

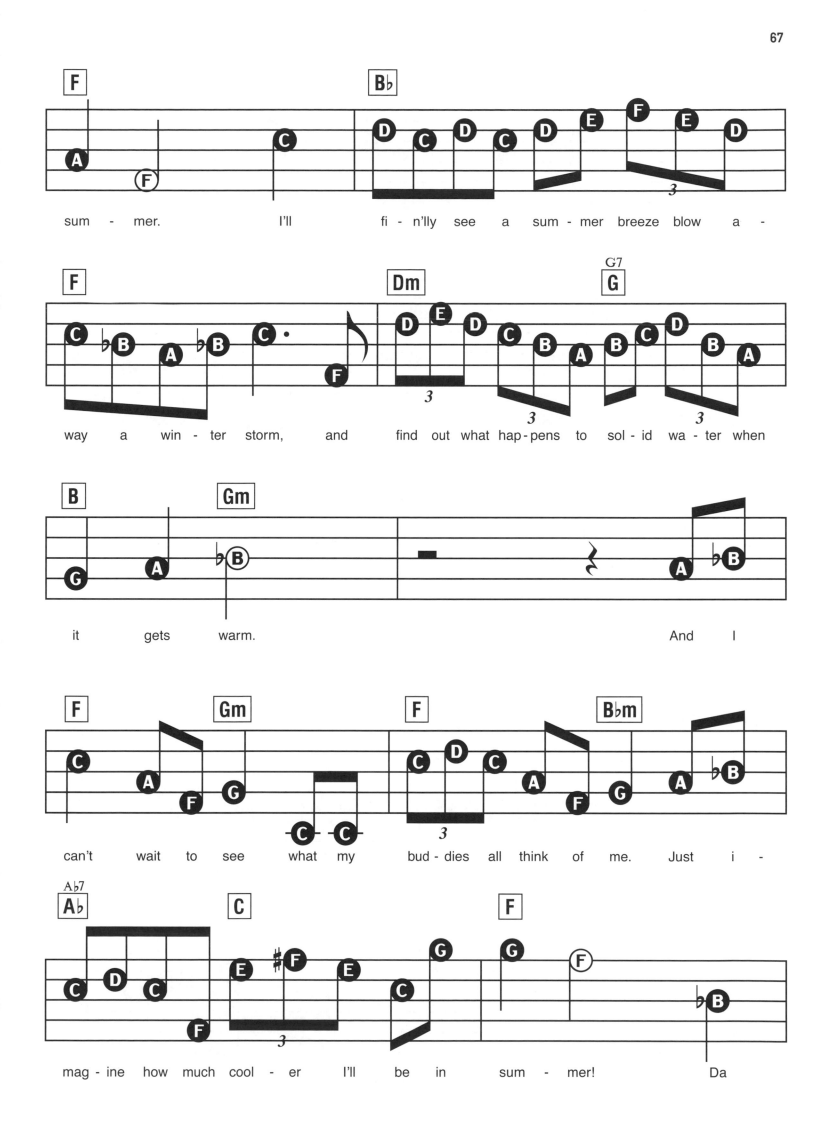

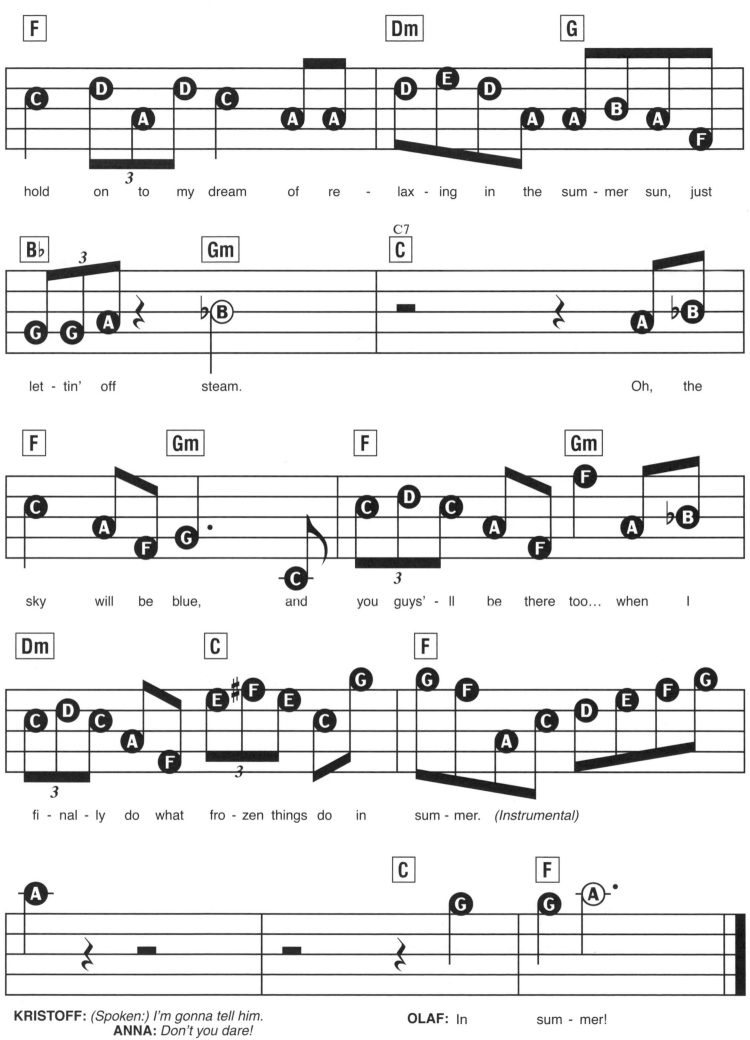

It's a Small World

from Disney Parks' "it's a small world" attraction

Registration 2
Rhythm: March

Words and Music by Richard M. Sherman
and Robert B. Sherman

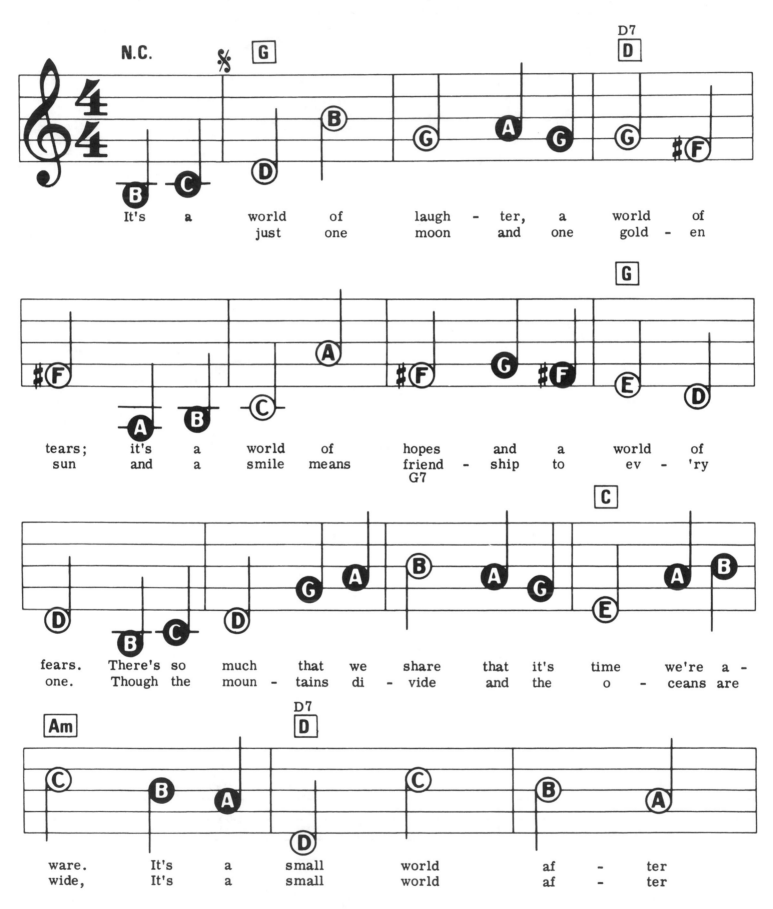

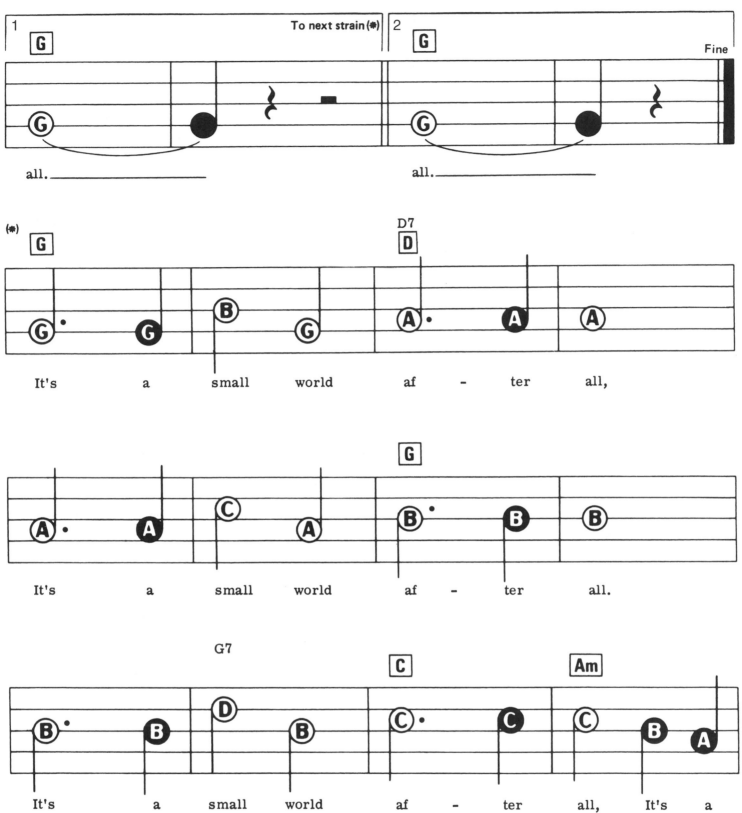

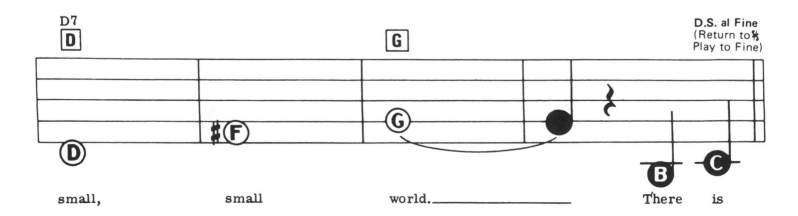

Lava
from LAVA

Registration 4
Rhythm: Folk or Swing

Music and Lyrics by
James Ford Murphy

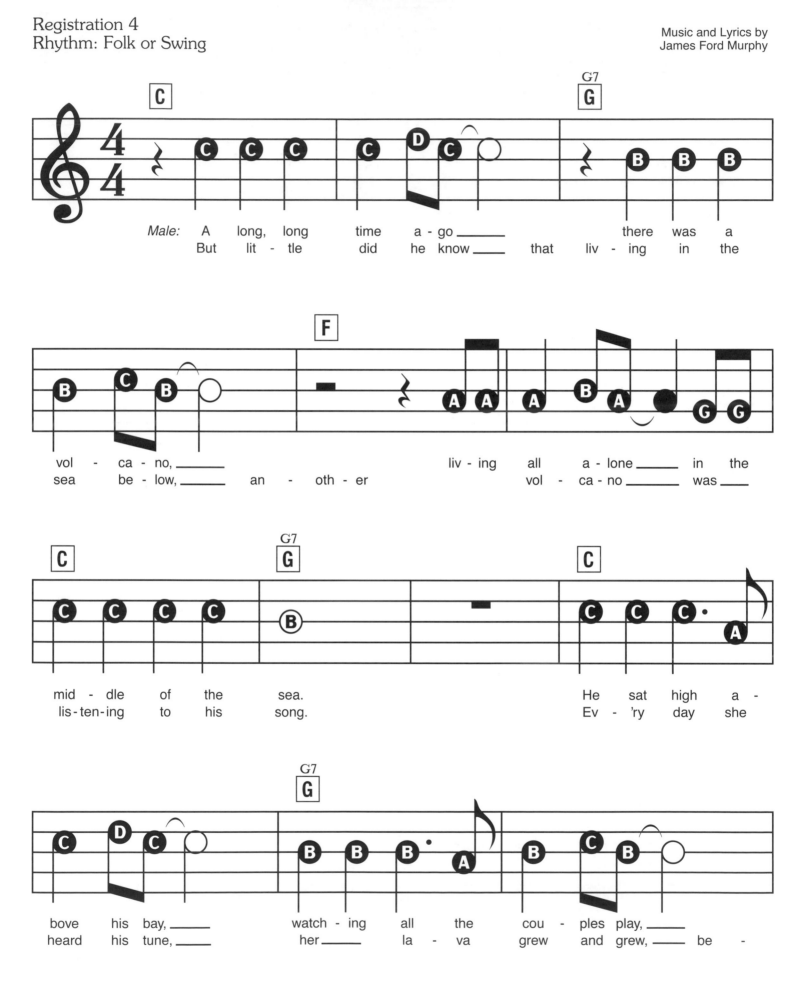

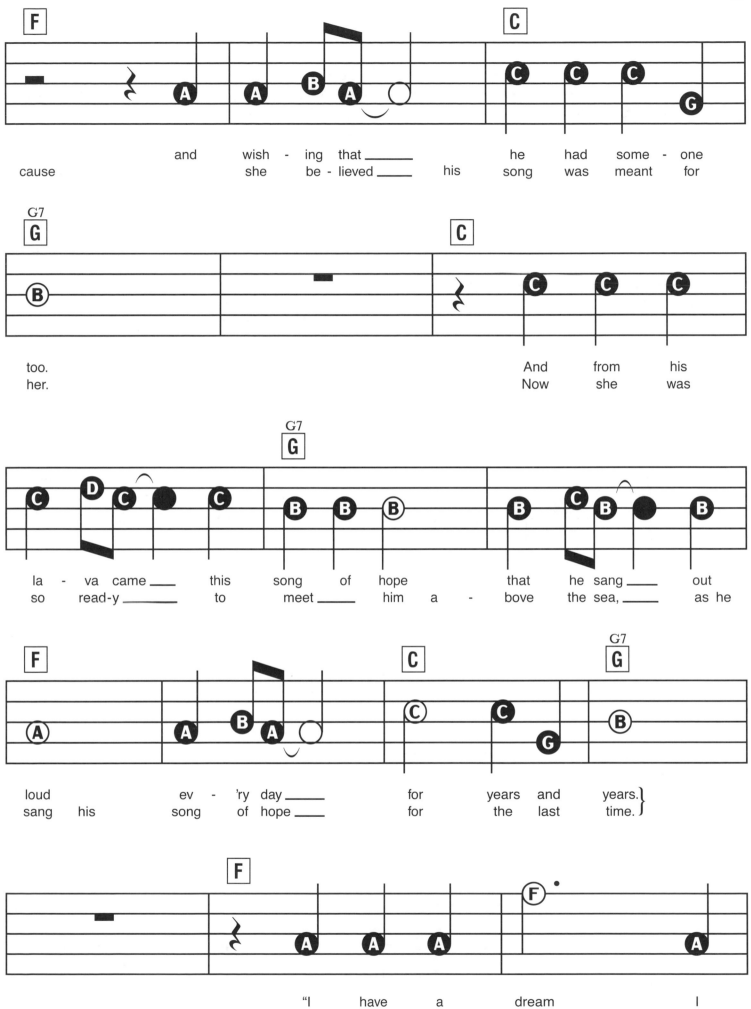

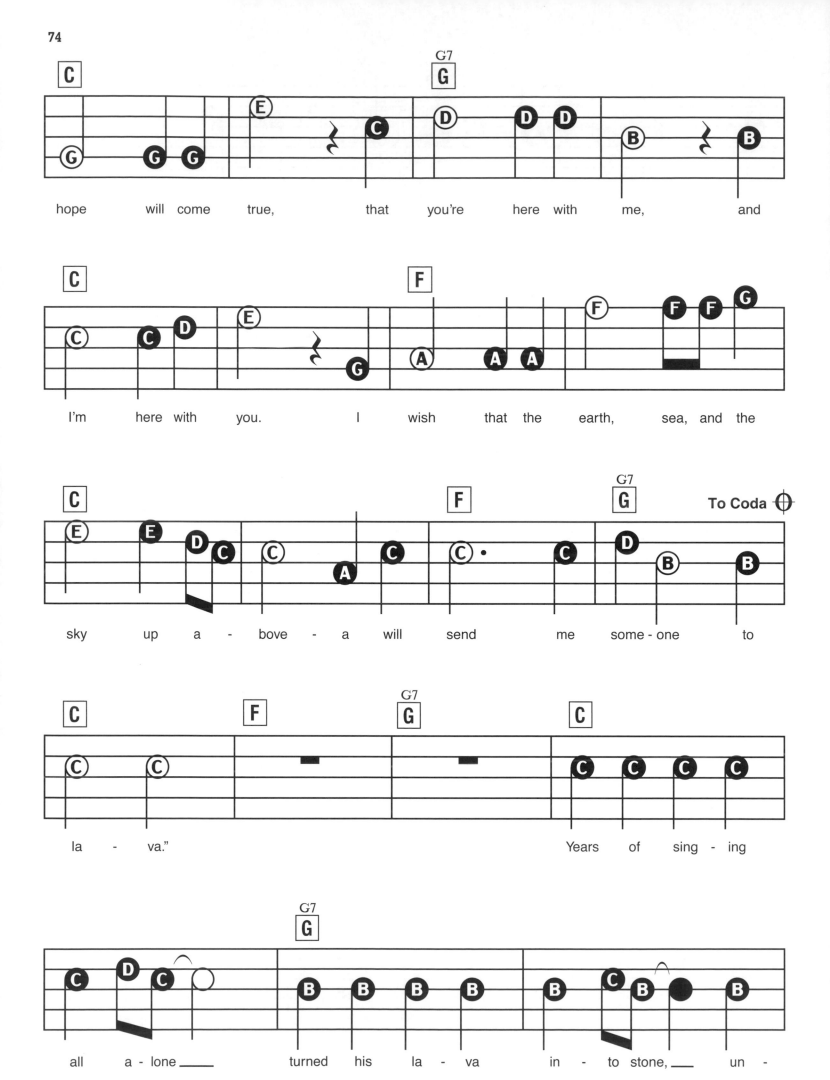

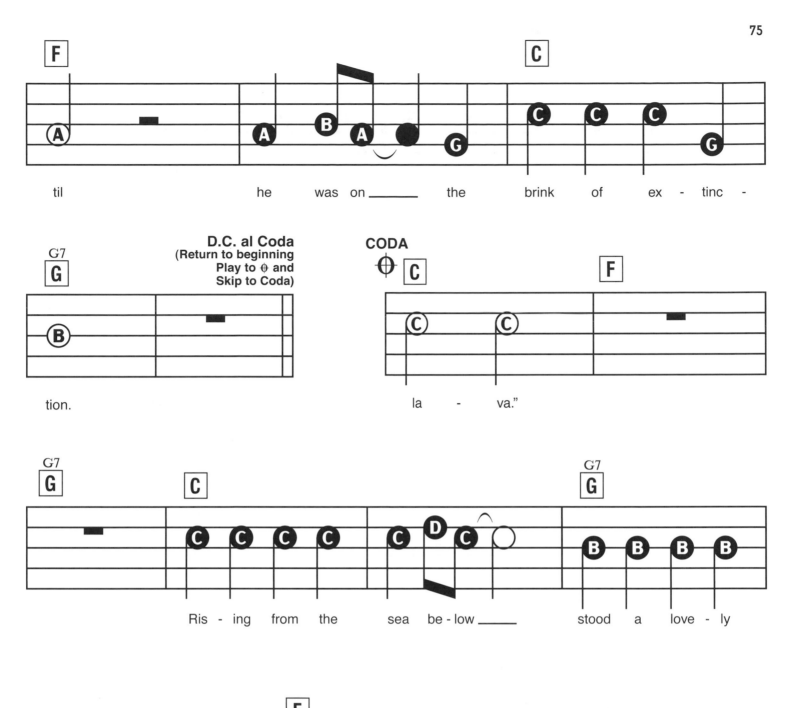

til   he was on _____ the   brink of ex - tinc -

D.C. al Coda
(Return to beginning
Play to ⊕ and
Skip to Coda)

CODA

tion.   la - va."

Ris - ing from the   sea be - low _____   stood a love - ly

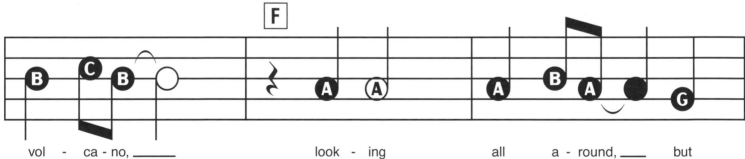

vol - ca - no, _____   look - ing   all a - round, ___ but

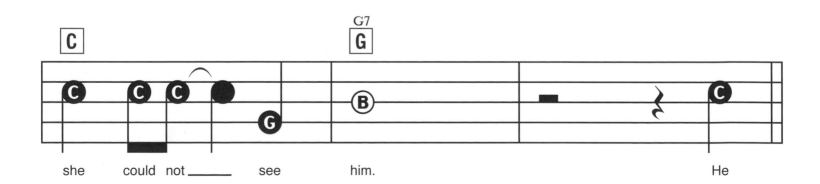

she could not _____ see   him.   He

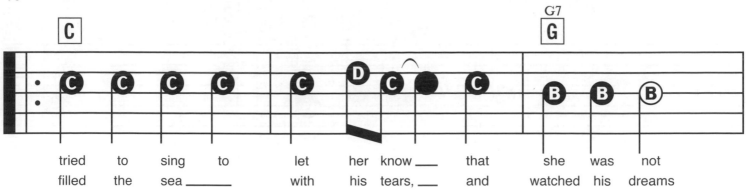

tried to sing to | let her know ____ that | she was not
filled the sea _____ | with his tears, ____ and | watched his dreams

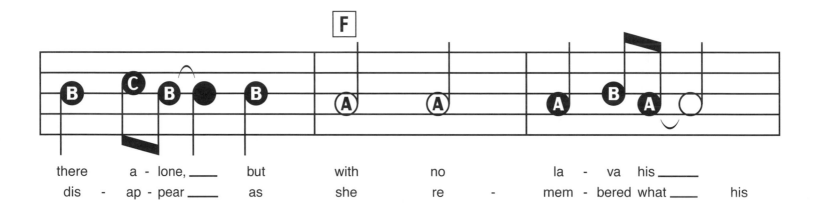

there a - lone, ____ but | with no | la - va his _____
dis - ap - pear ____ as | she re - | mem - bered what ____ his

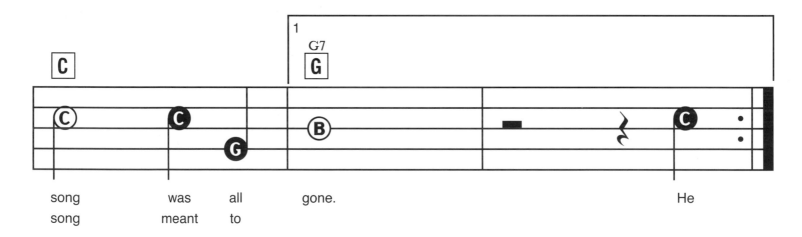

song was all gone. | He
song meant to

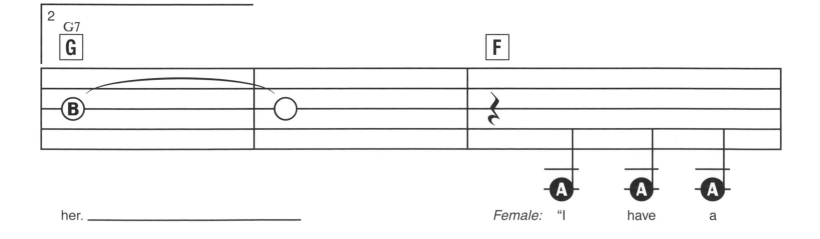

her. _____ | *Female:* "I have a

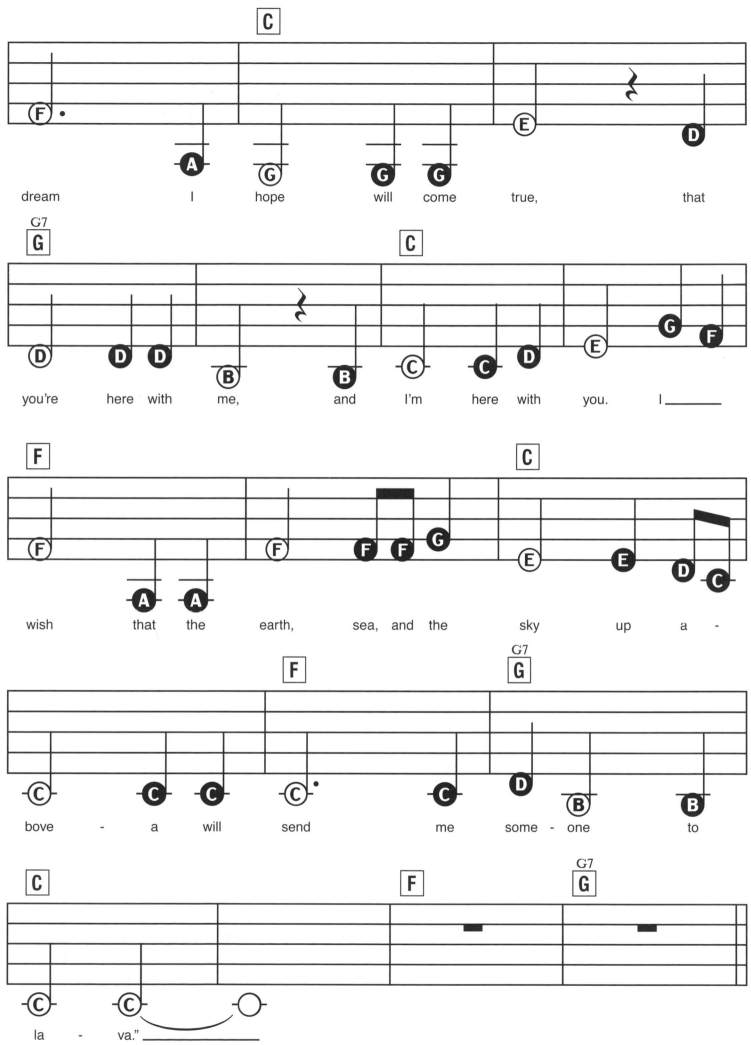

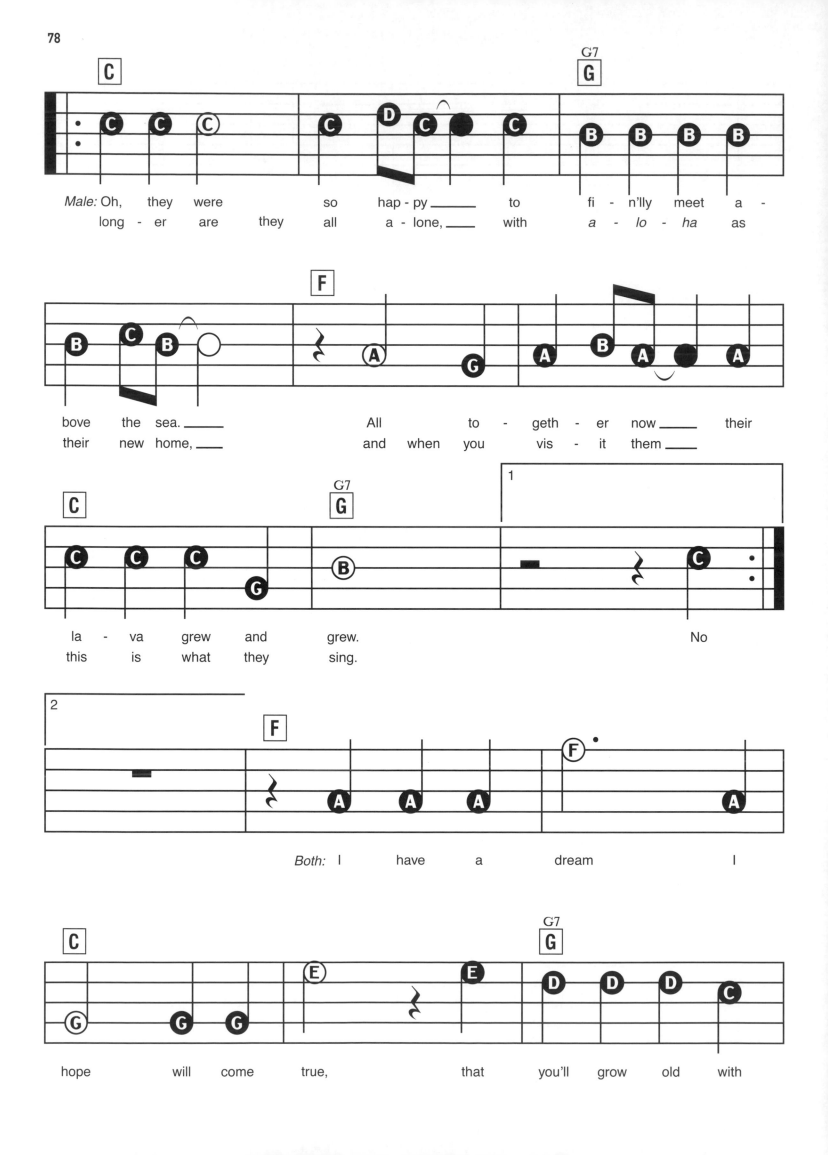

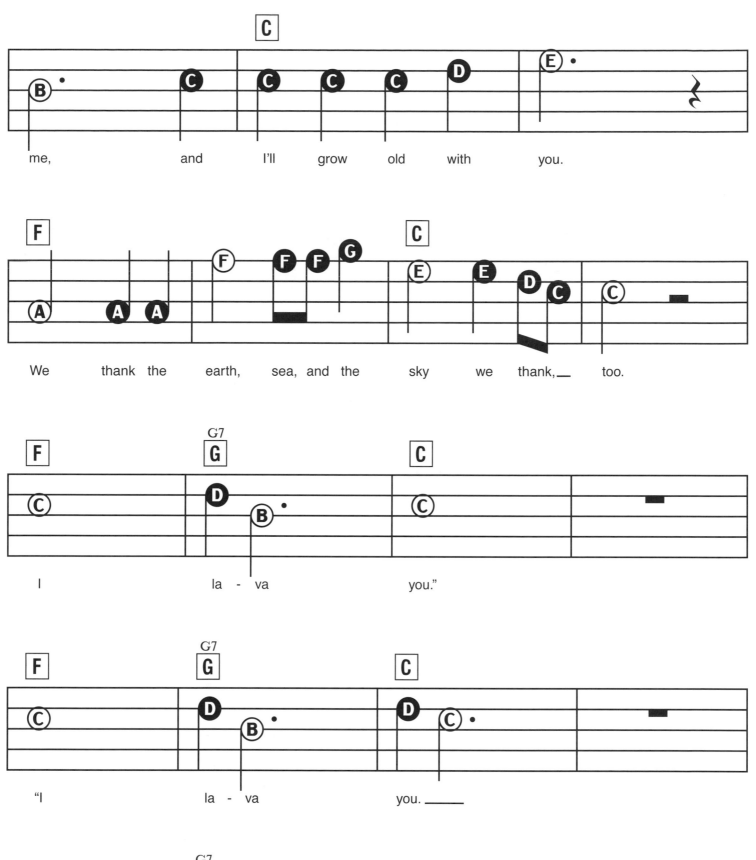

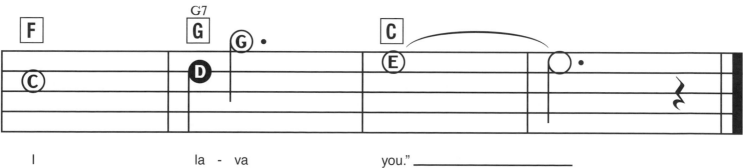

One Jump Ahead
from ALADDIN

Registration 5
Rhythm: Polka

Words by Tim Rice
Music by Alan Menken

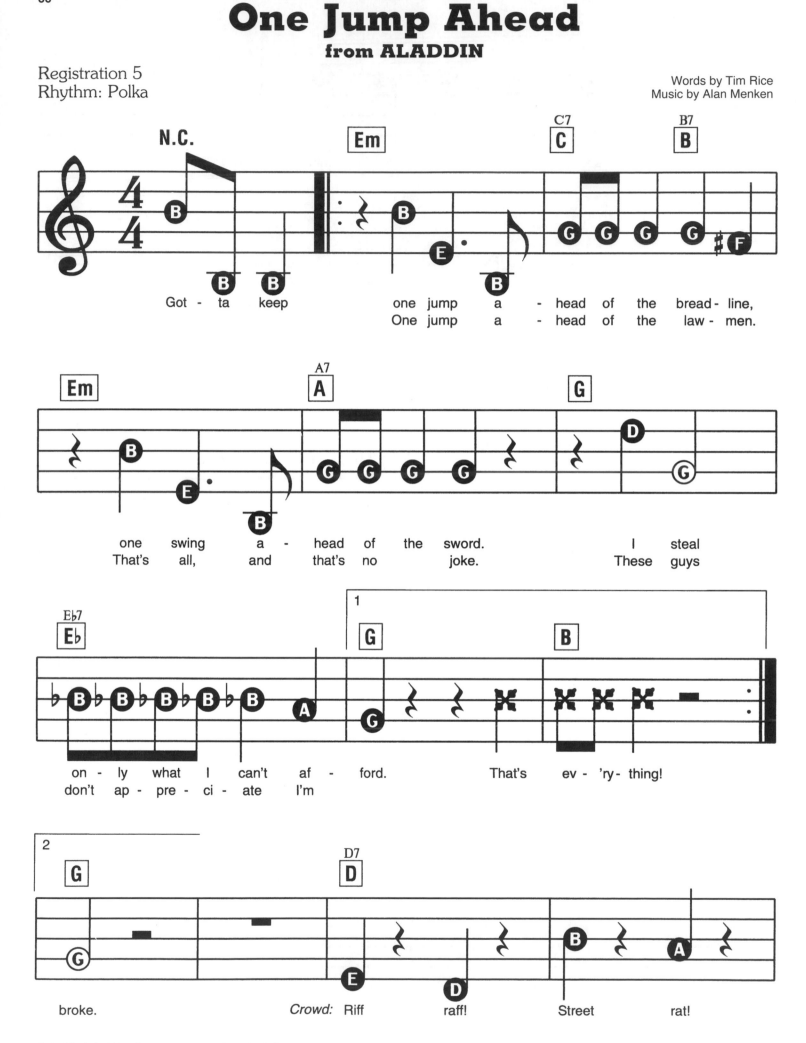

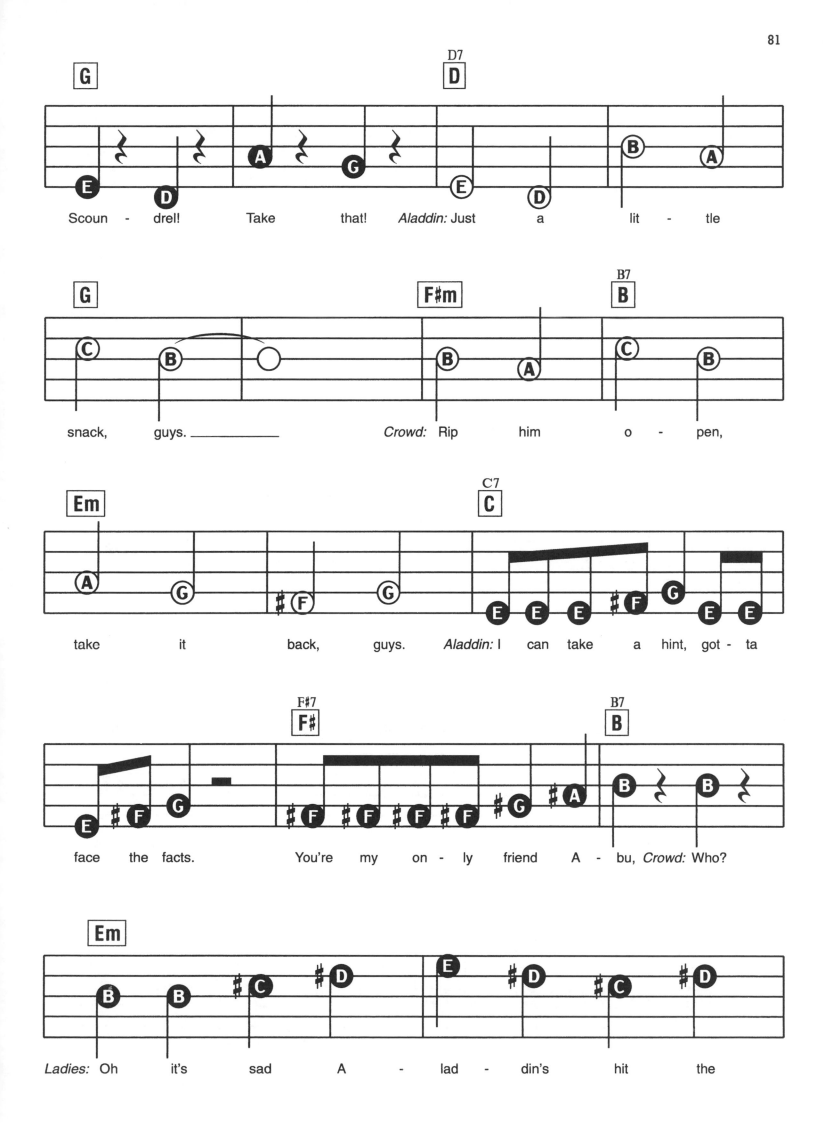

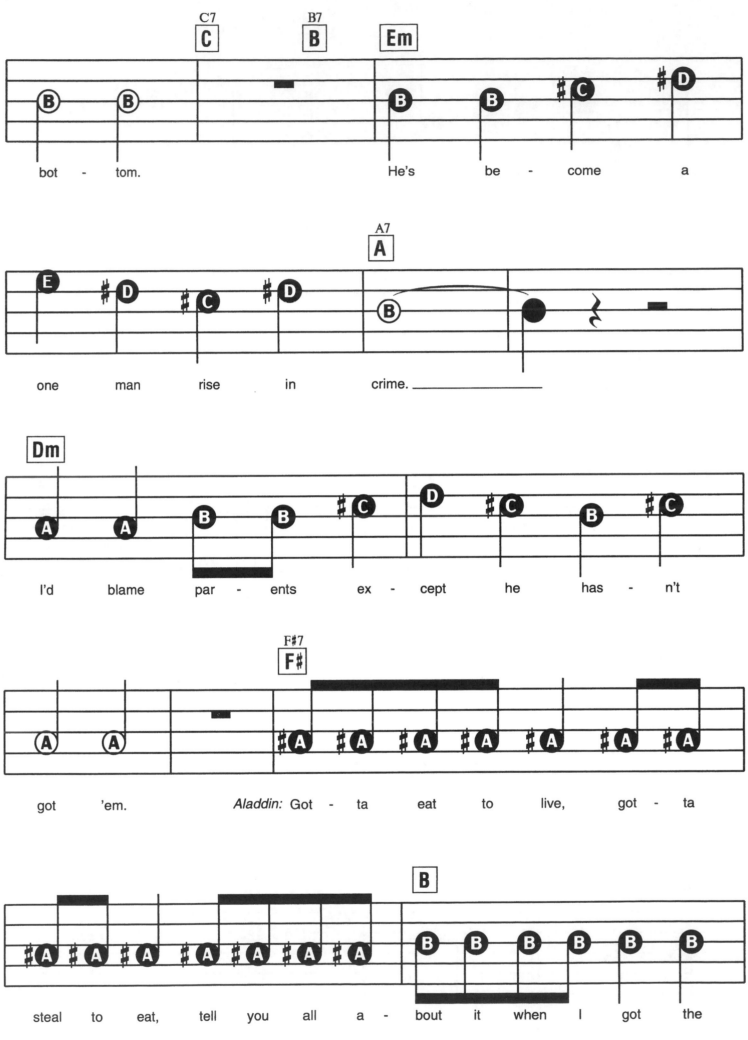

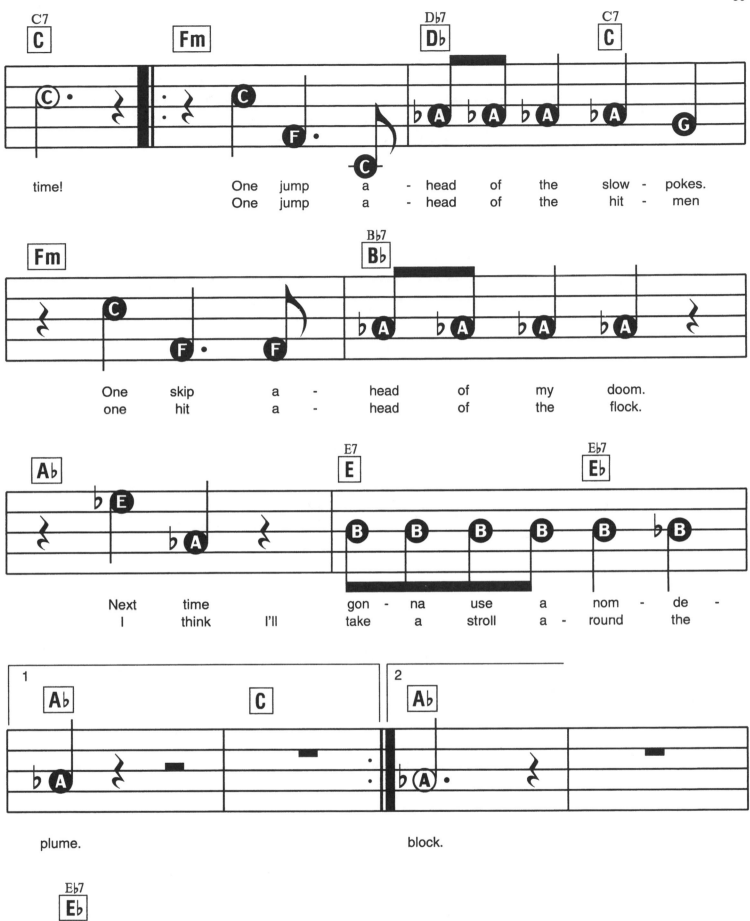

time!

One jump a - head of the slow - pokes.
One jump a - head of the hit - men

One skip a - head of my doom.
one hit a - head of the flock.

Next time I gon - na use a nom - de -
I think I'll take a use stroll a - round the

plume.
block.

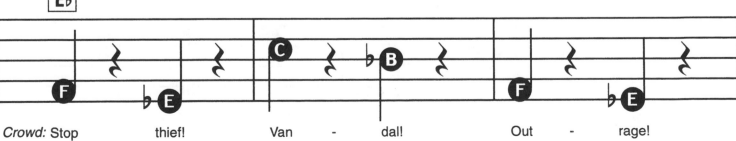

Crowd: Stop thief! Van - dal! Out - rage!

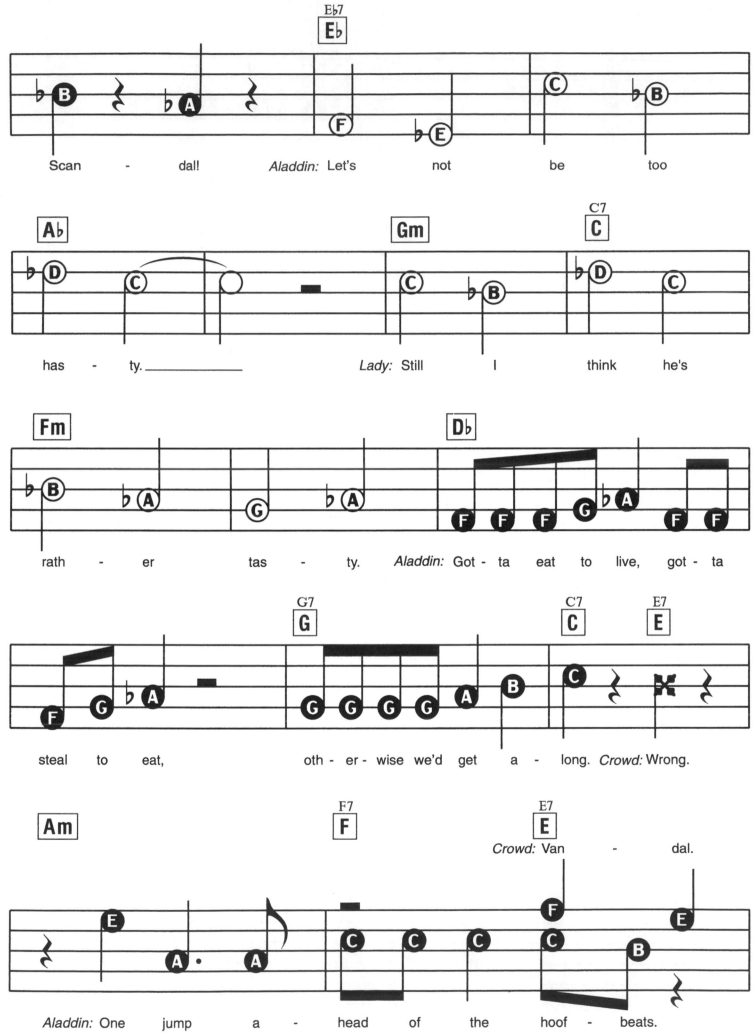

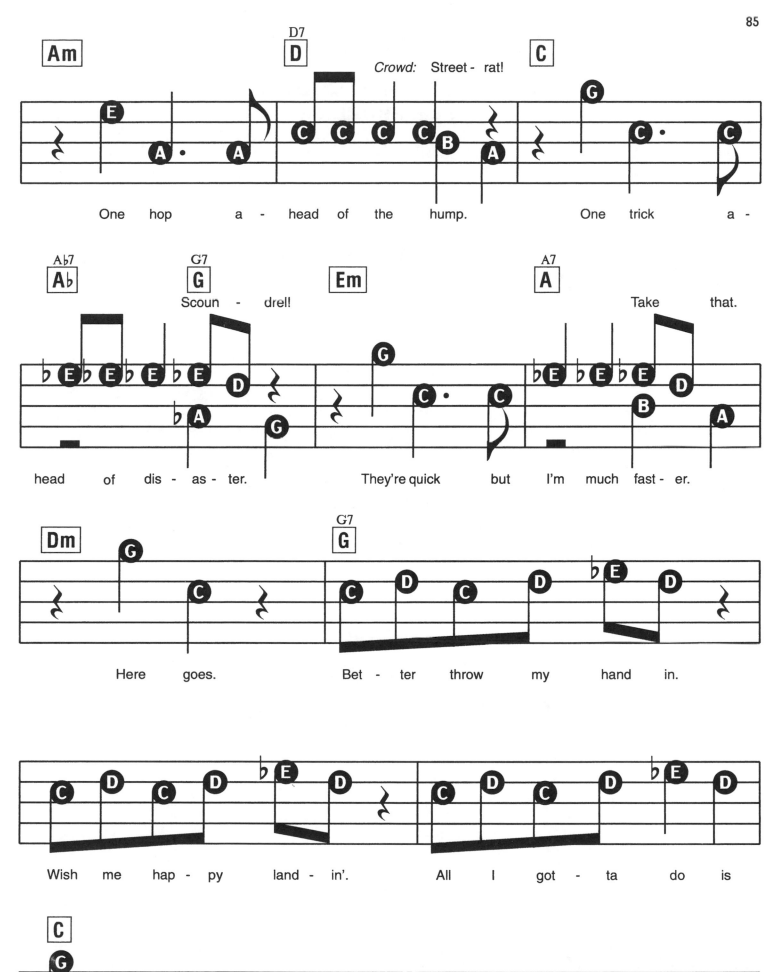

Reindeer(s) Are Better Than People

from FROZEN

Registration 4
Rhythm: Waltz

Music and Lyrics by Kristen Anderson-Lopez
and Robert Lopez

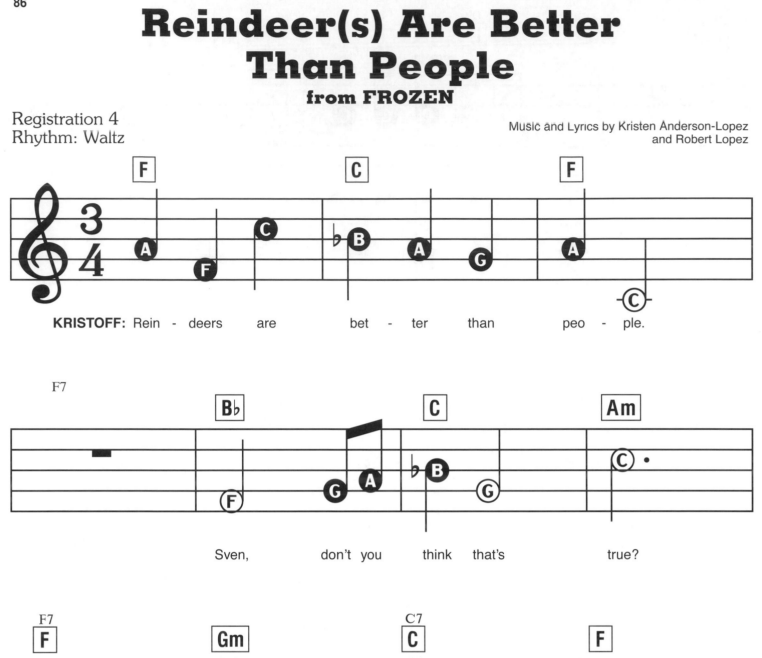

KRISTOFF: Rein - deers are bet - ter than peo - ple.

Sven, don't you think that's true?

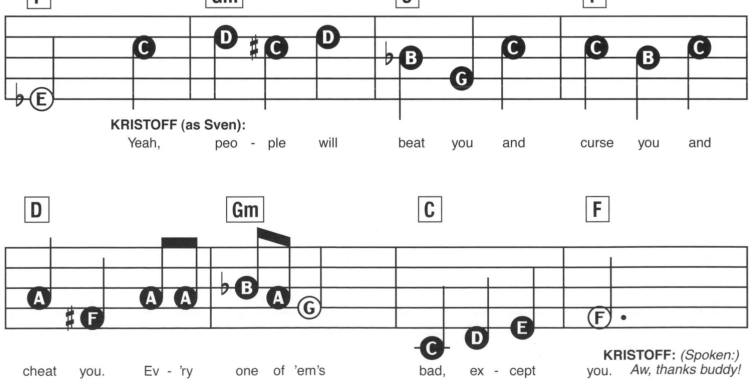

KRISTOFF (as Sven):
Yeah, peo - ple will beat you and curse you and

cheat you. Ev - 'ry one of 'em's bad, ex - cept you.

KRISTOFF: (Spoken:)
Aw, thanks buddy!

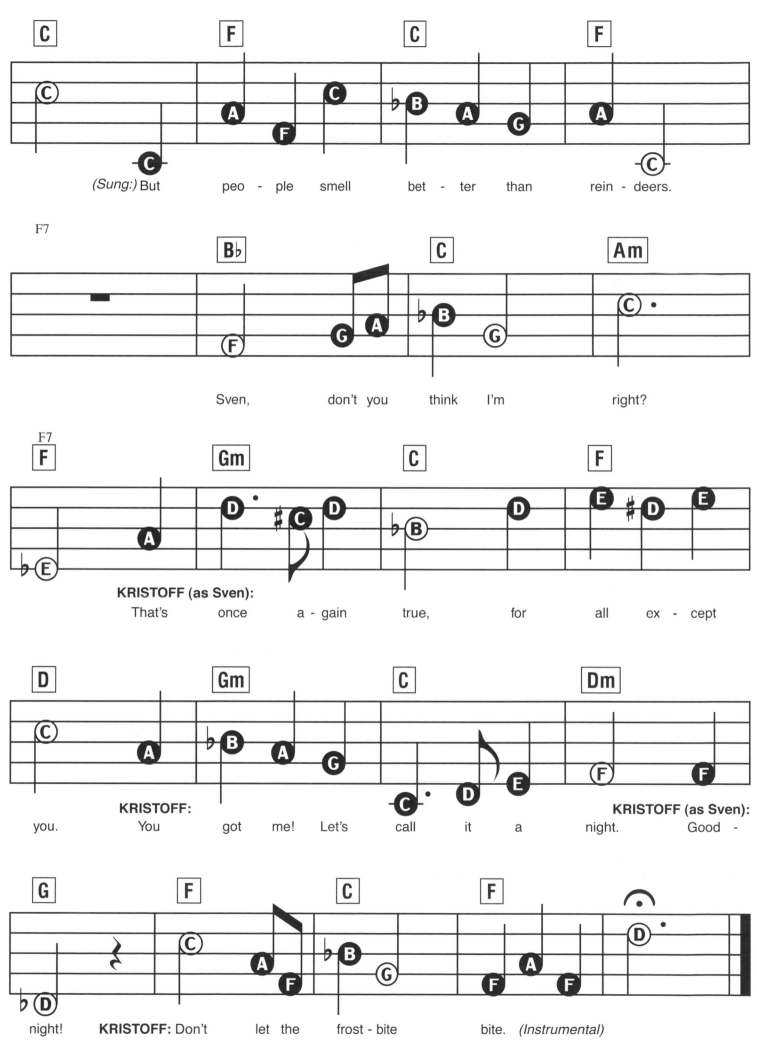

A Spoonful of Sugar
from MARY POPPINS

Registration 3
Rhythm: Fox Trot or Swing

Words and Music by Richard M. Sherman
and Robert B. Sherman

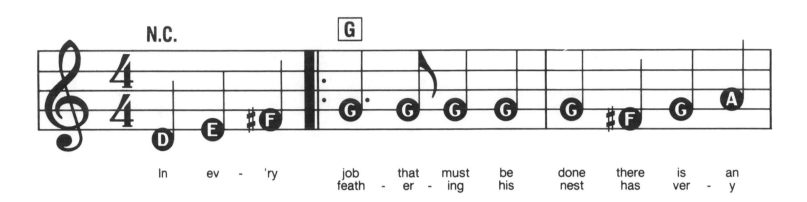

In ev - 'ry job that must be done there is an
feath - er - ing his done nest has ver - y

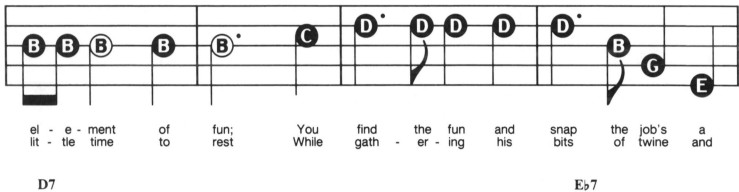

el - e - ment of fun; You find the fun and snap the job's a
lit - tle time to rest While find gath - er - ing his bits of twine and

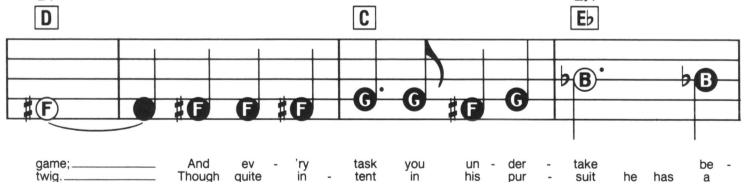

game;_____ And ev - 'ry task you un - der - take be -
twig._____ Though quite in - tent in his pur - suit he has a

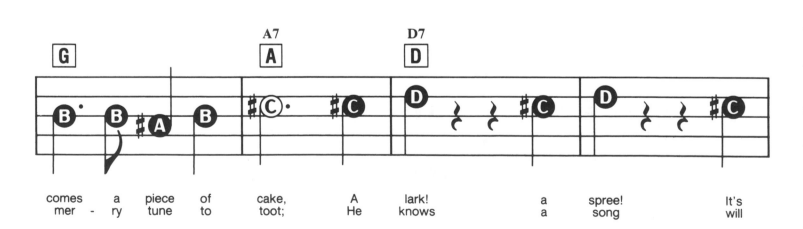

comes a piece of cake, A lark! a spree! It's
mer - ry tune to toot; He knows a song It will

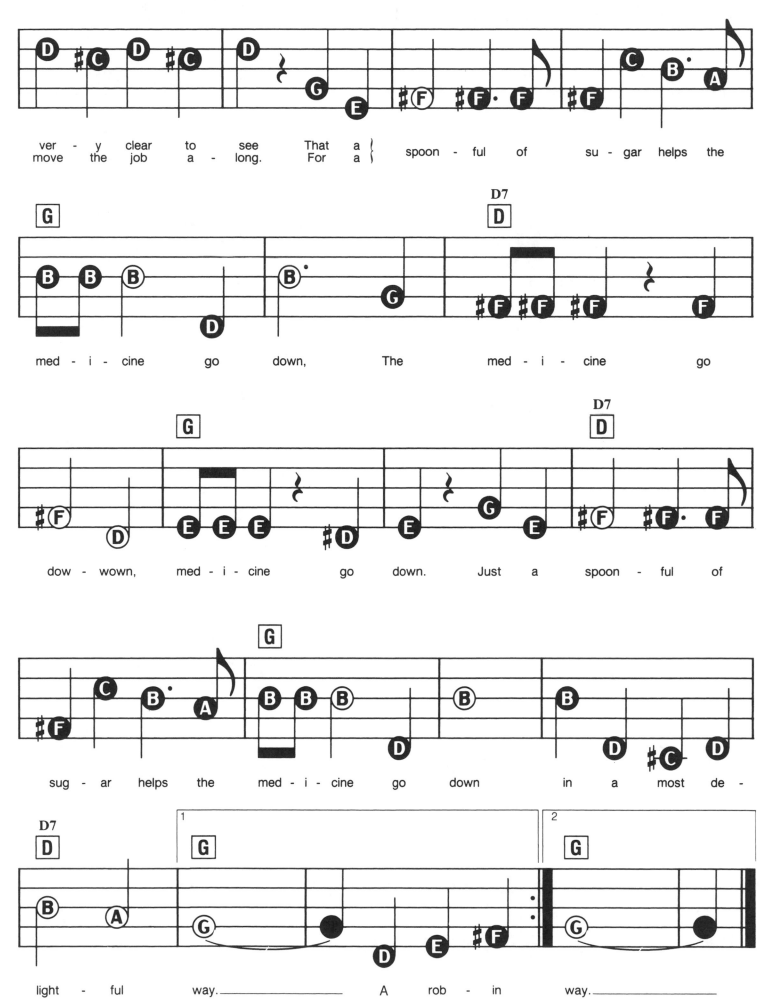

Supercalifragilisticexpialidocious
from MARY POPPINS

Registration 2
Rhythm: Fox Trot or Swing

Words and Music by Richard M. Sherman
and Robert B. Sherman

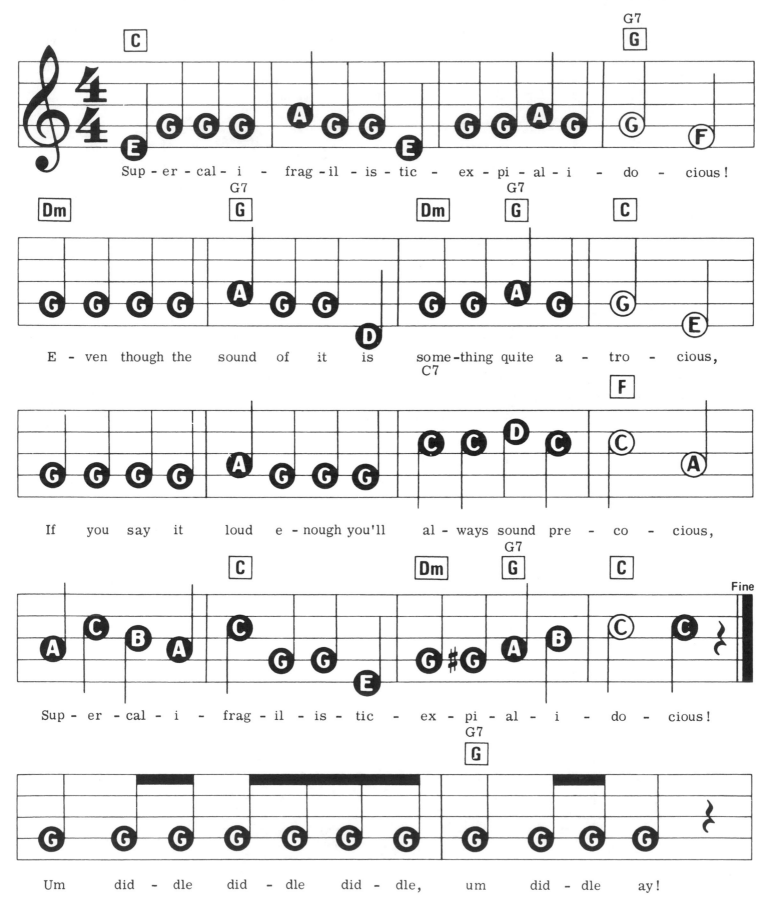

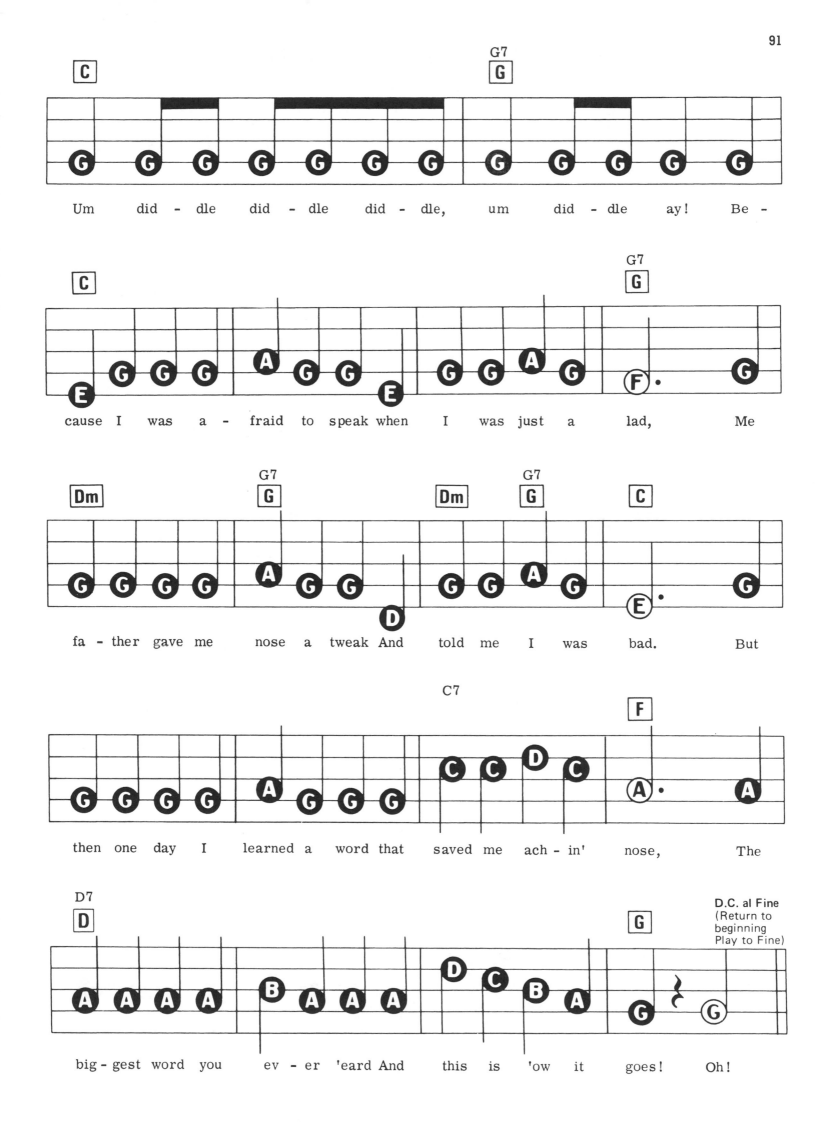

The Unbirthday Song
from ALICE IN WONDERLAND

Registration 2
Rhythm: Ballad or Fox Trot

Words and Music by Mack David,
Al Hoffman and Jerry Livingston

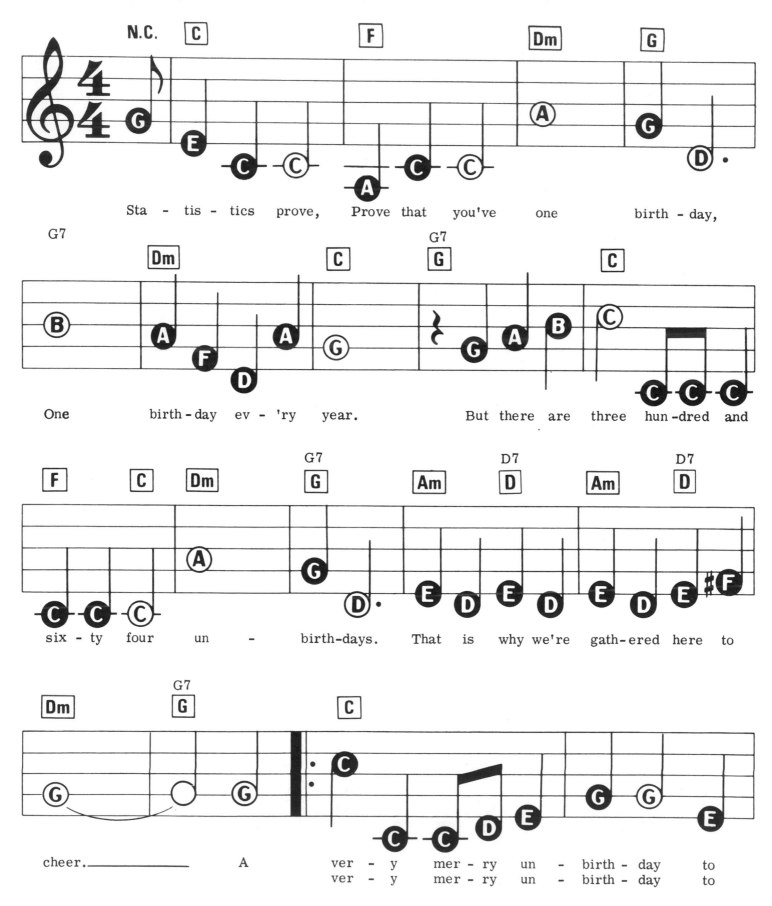

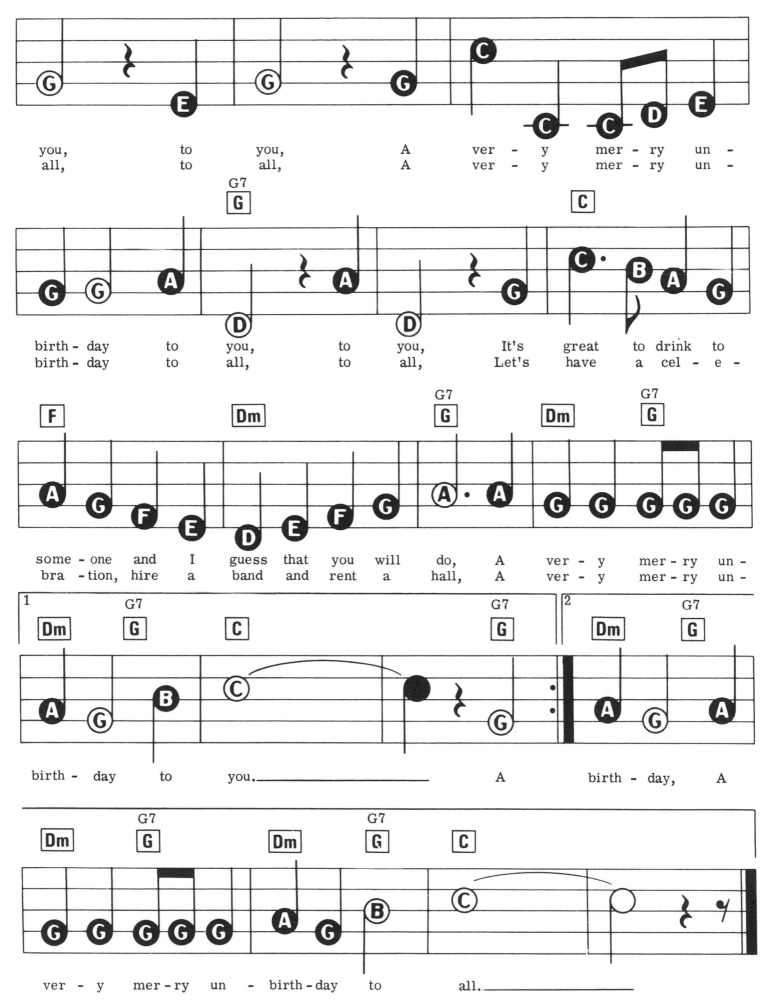

Under the Sea
from THE LITTLE MERMAID

Registration 7
Rhythm: Bossa Nova or Latin

Music by Alan Menken
Lyrics by Howard Ashman

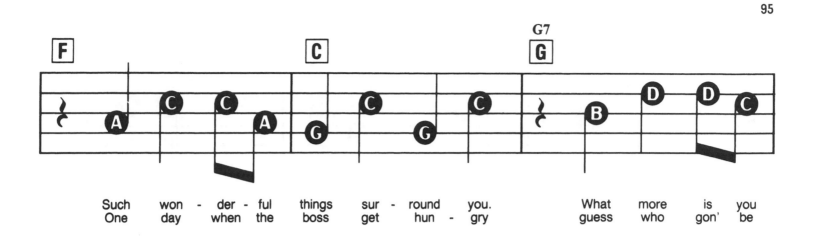

Such won - der - ful things sur - round you. What more is you
One day when the boss get hun - gry guess who is gon' be

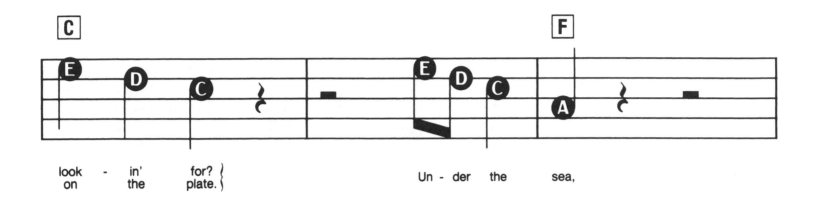

look - in' for? Un - der the sea,
on the plate.

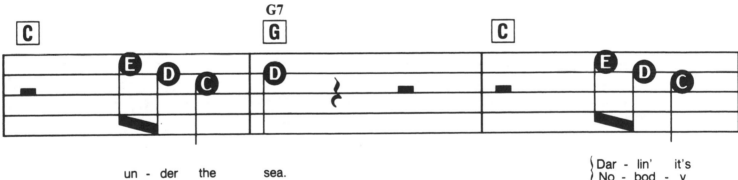

un - der the sea. Dar - lin' it's
No - bod - y

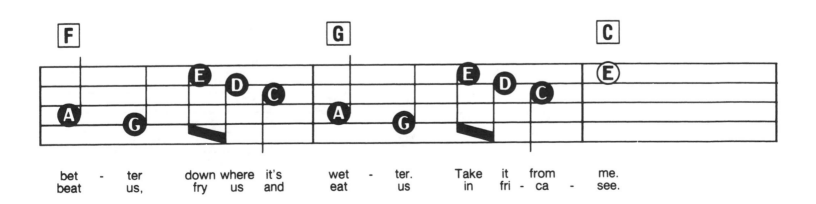

bet - ter, down where it's wet - ter. Take it from me.
beat us, fry us and eat us in fri - ca - see.

Up on the shore they work all day.
We what the land folks loves to cook.

Out in the
Un - der the

sun they slave a - way.
sea we off the hook.

While we de - vo - tin' full - time to
We got no trou - bles, life is the

float - in' un - der the sea.
bub - bles un - der the

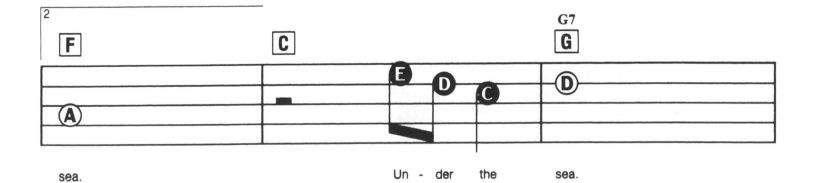

sea.

Un - der the sea.

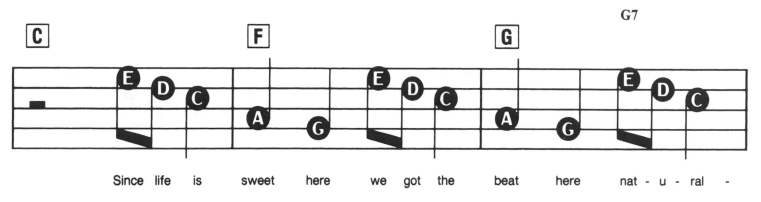

Since life is sweet here we got the beat here nat - u - ral -

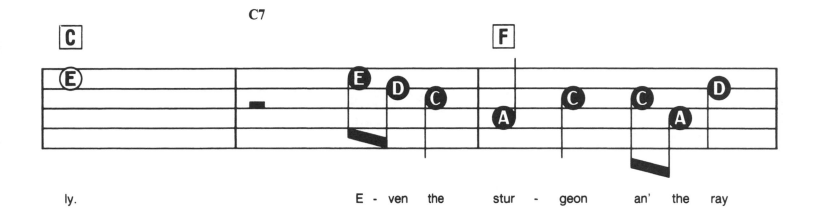

ly.   E - ven the stur - geon an' the ray

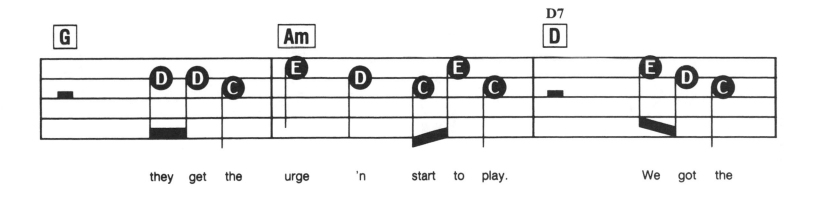

they get the urge 'n start to play.   We got the

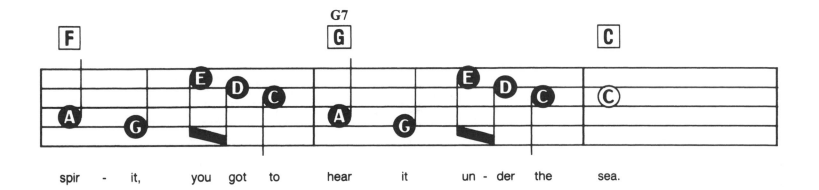

spir - it, you got to hear it un - der the sea.

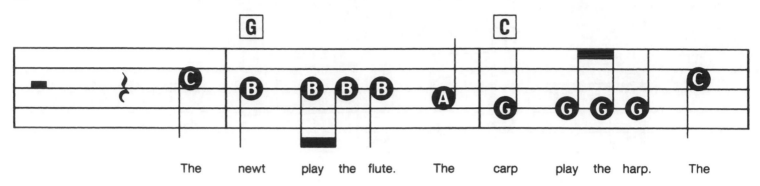

The newt play the flute. The carp play the harp. The

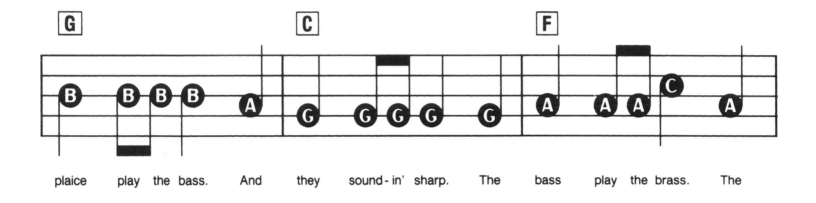

plaice play the bass. And they sound-in' sharp. The bass play the brass. The

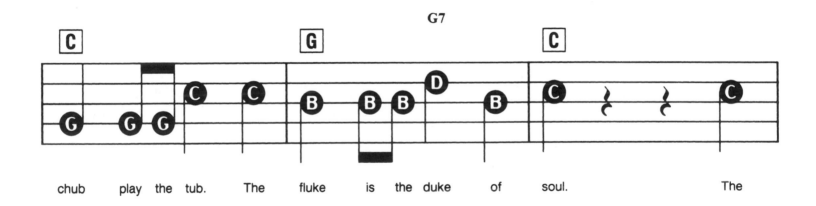

chub play the tub. The fluke is the duke of soul. The

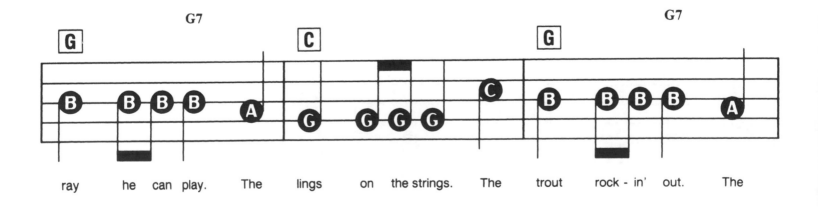

ray he can play. The lings on the strings. The trout rock-in' out. The

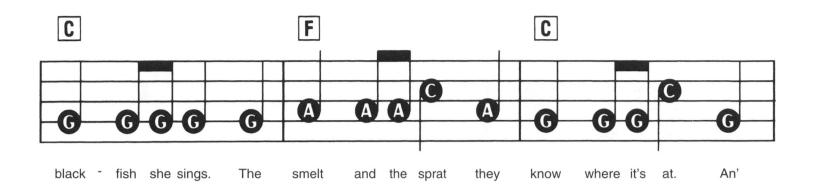

black - fish she sings. The smelt and the sprat they know where it's at. An'

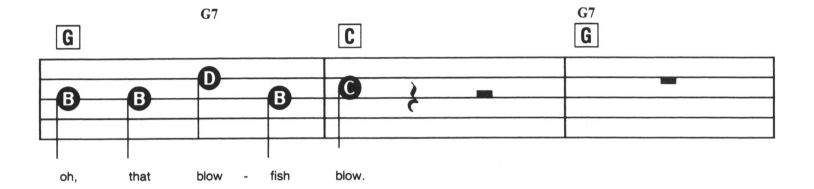

oh, that blow - fish blow.

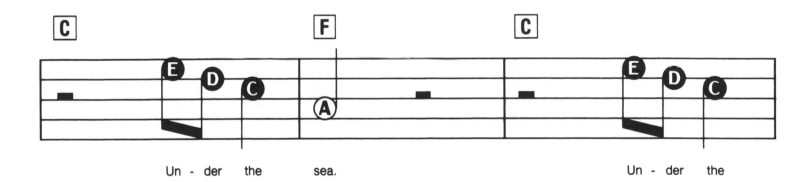

Un - der the sea. Un - der the

G7
G   C   F

sea. When the sar - dine be - gin the be -

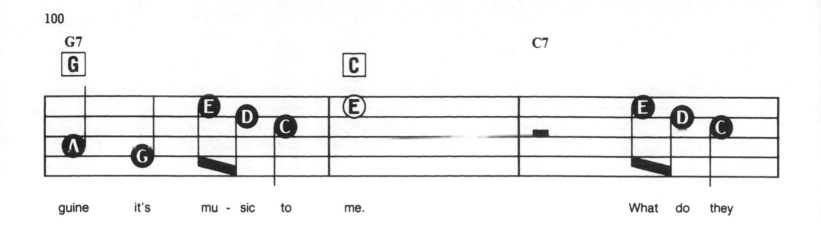

guine it's mu - sic to me. What do they

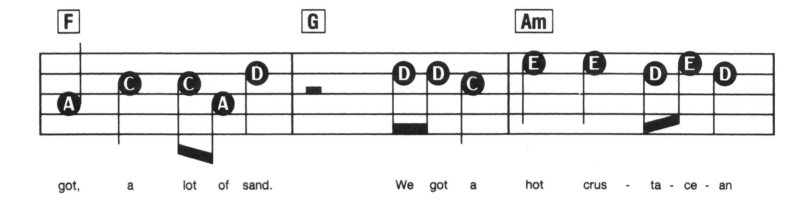

got, a lot of sand. We got a hot crus - ta - ce - an

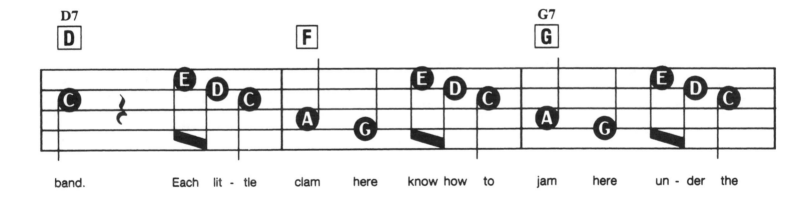

band. Each lit - tle clam here know how to jam here un - der the

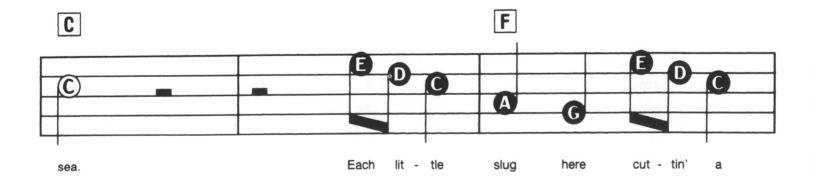

sea. Each lit - tle slug here cut - tin' a

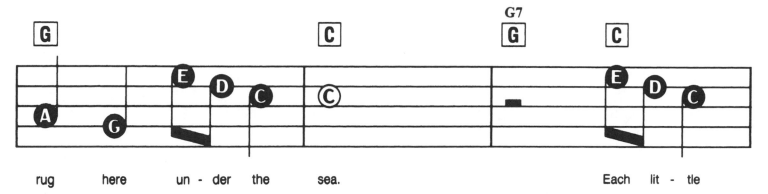

rug here un-der the sea. Each lit - tle

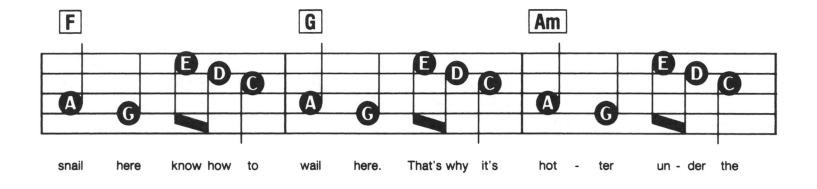

snail here know how to wail here. That's why it's hot - ter un - der the

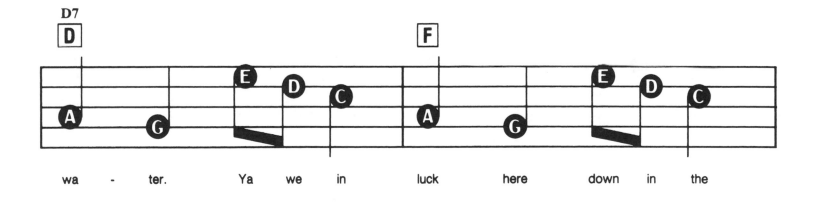

wa - ter. Ya we in luck here down in the

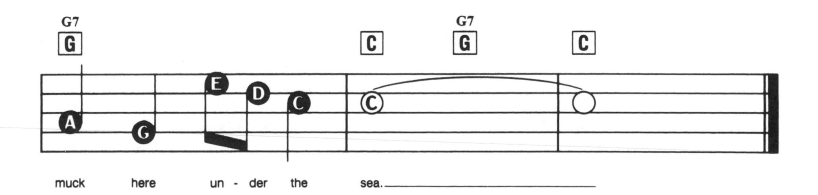

muck here un - der the sea.

When I See an Elephant Fly

from DUMBO

Registration 8
Rhythm: Fox Trot or Swing

Words by Ned Washington
Music by Oliver Wallace

I saw a pea- nut stand, heard a rub- ber band, I saw a
front porch swing, heard a dia- mond ring, I saw a

nee- dle that winked it's eye,
pol- ka- dot rail- road tie,
But I think I will have seen

ev- 'ry- thing when I see an el- e- phant fly. I saw a

fly. I ev- en heard a choc o- late drop, I

went in- to a store, saw a bi- cy- cle shop.

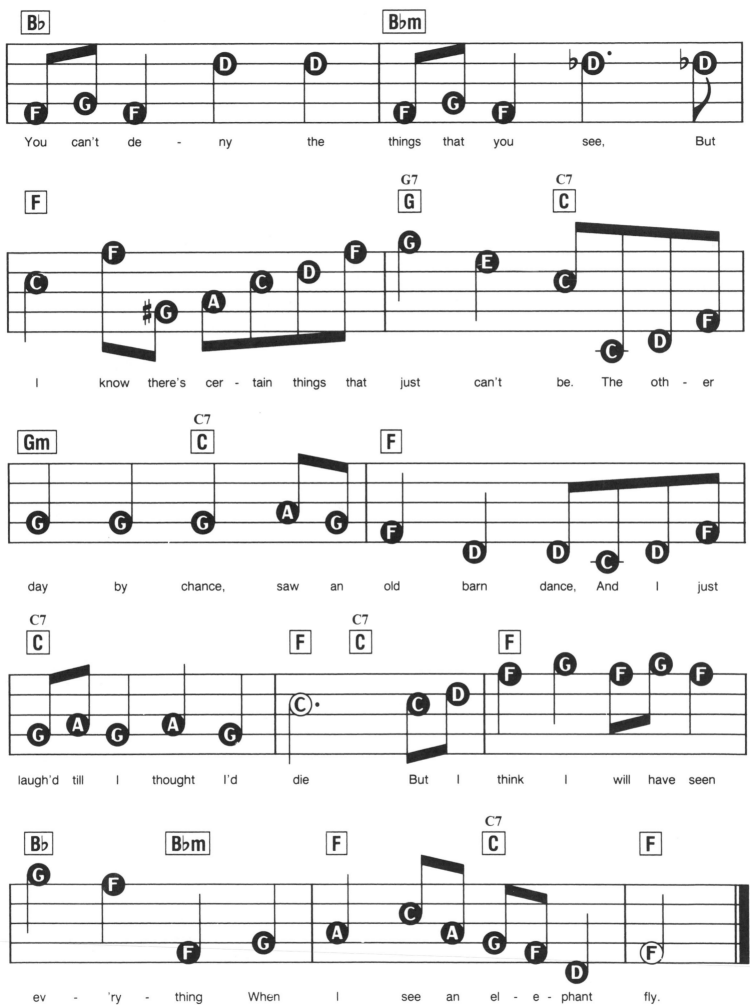

Whistle While You Work
from SNOW WHITE AND THE SEVEN DWARFS

Registration 2
Rhythm: Fox Trot or Swing

Words by Larry Morey
Music by Frank Chruchill

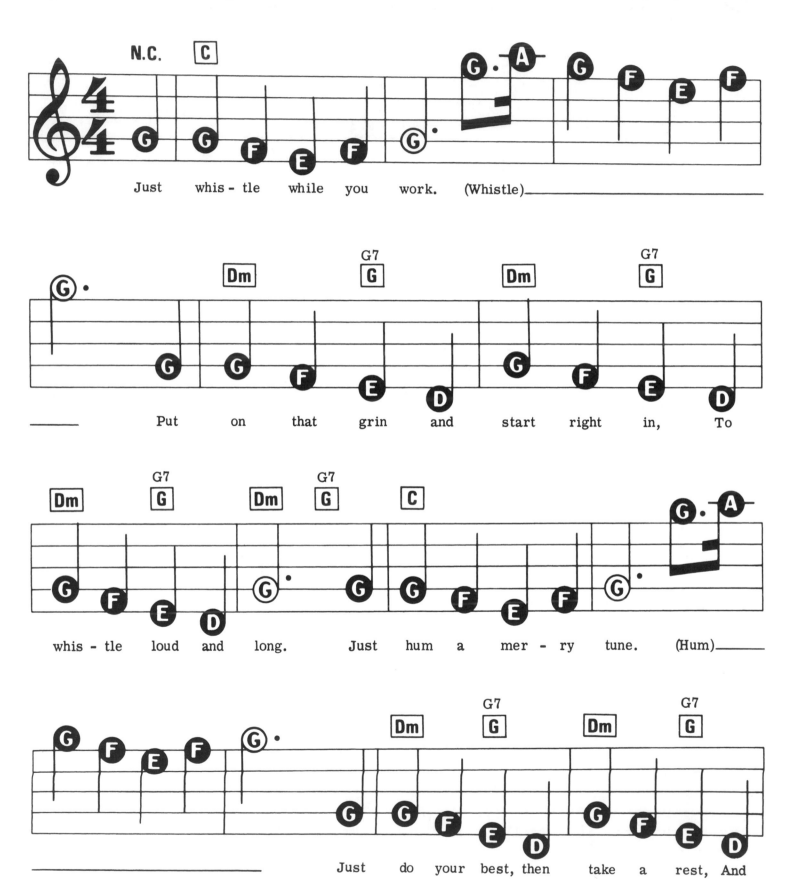

Who's Afraid of the Big Bad Wolf?

from THREE LITTLE PIGS

Registration 4
Rhythm: Fox Trot or Swing

Words and Music by Frank Churchill
Additional Lyric by Ann Ronell

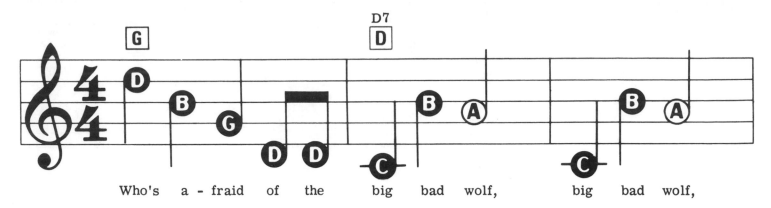

Who's a - fraid of the big bad wolf, big bad wolf,

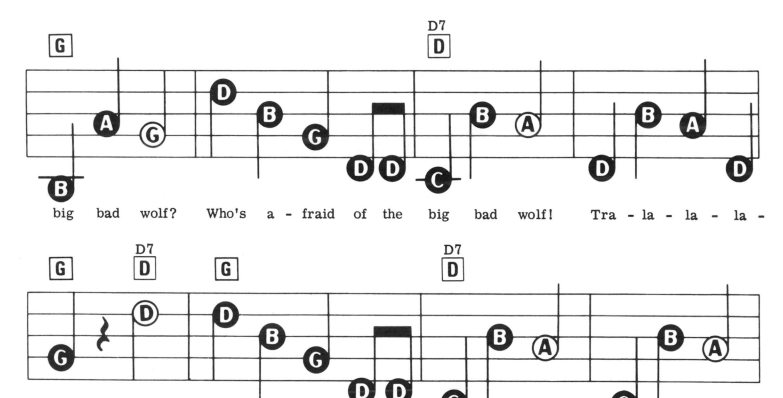

big bad wolf? Who's a - fraid of the big bad wolf! Tra - la - la - la - la.

Who's a - fraid of the big bad wolf, big bad wolf,

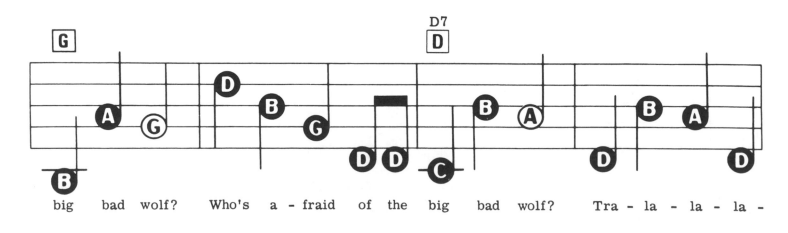

big bad wolf? Who's a - fraid of the big bad wolf? Tra - la - la - la -

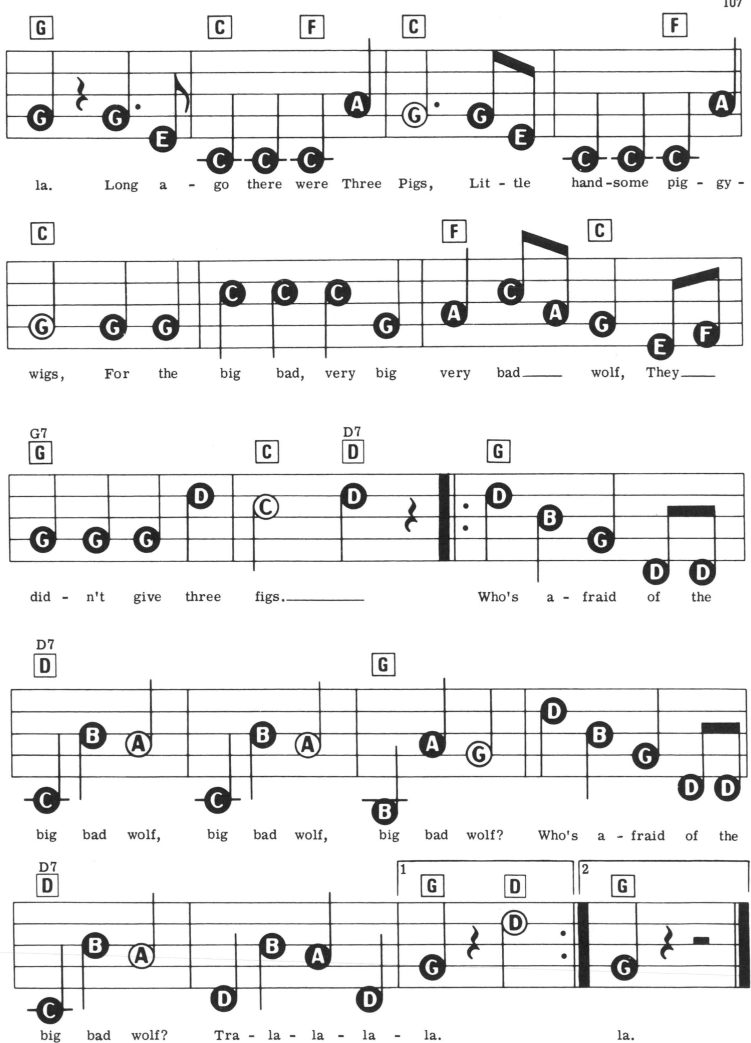

The Wonderful Thing About Tiggers*

from THE MANY ADVENTURES OF WINNIE THE POOH

Registration 1
Rhythm: Waltz

Words and Music by Richard M. Sherman
and Robert B. Sherman

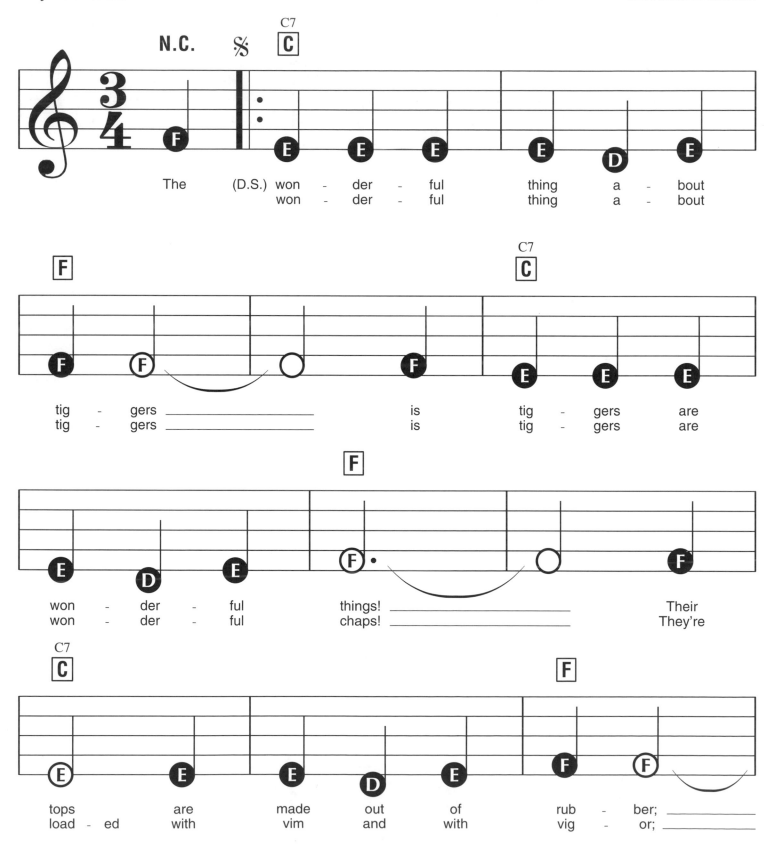

*Based on the "Winnie the Pooh" works, by A.A. Milne and E.H. Shepard

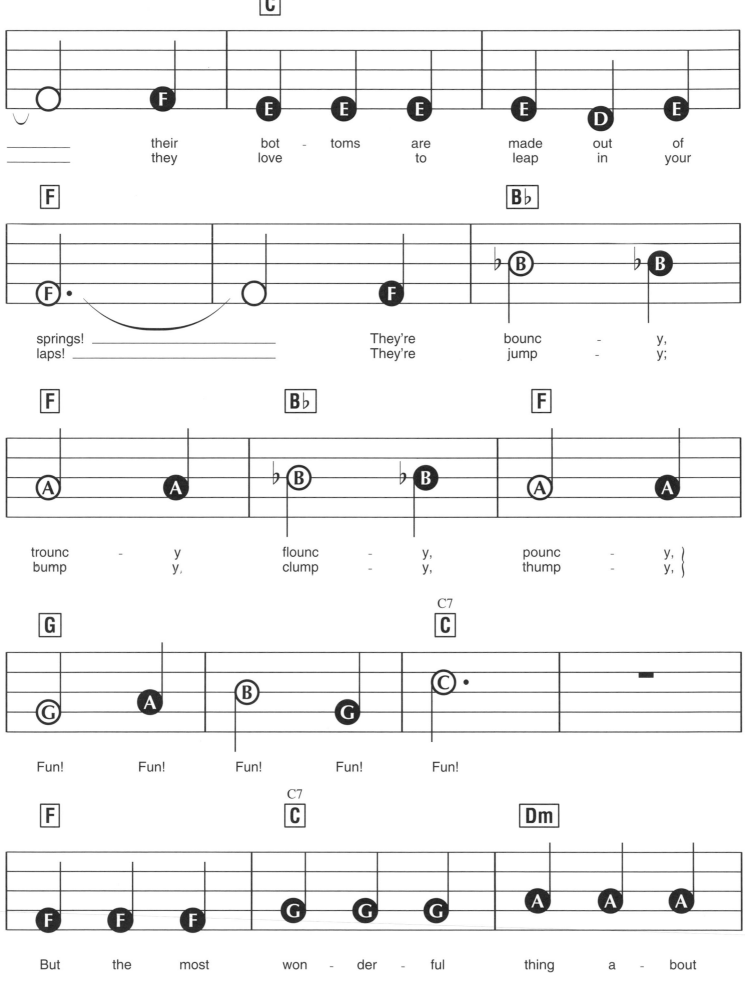

their bot - toms are made out of
they love to leap in your

springs! _____
laps! _____

They're bounc - y,
They're jump - y;

trounc - y
bump y,

flounc - y,
clump - y,

pounc - y,
thump - y,

Fun! Fun! Fun! Fun! Fun!

But the most won - der - ful thing a - bout

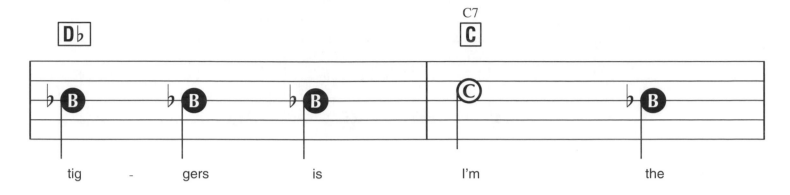

tig - gers is I'm the

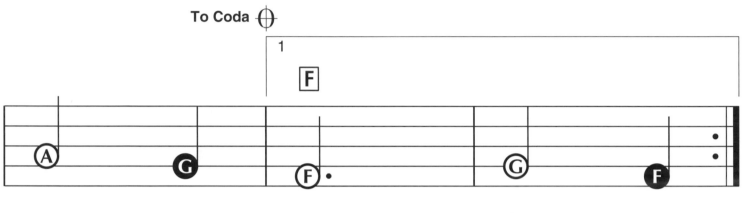

on - ly one! Oh, the

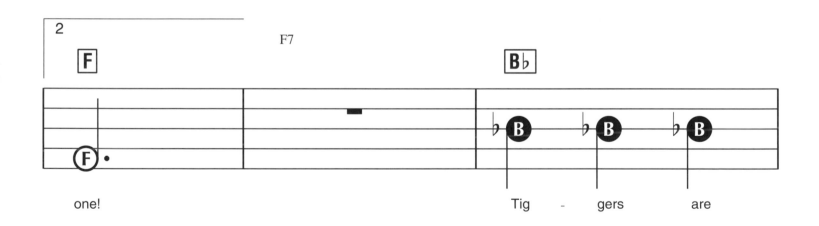

one! Tig - gers are

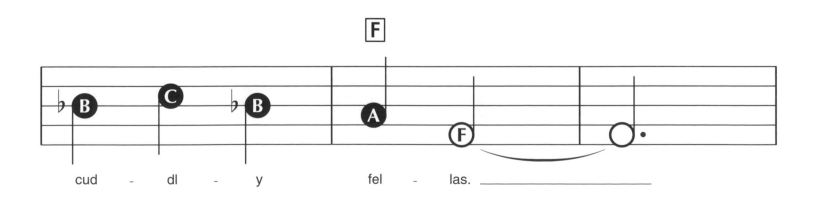

cud - dl - y fel - las.

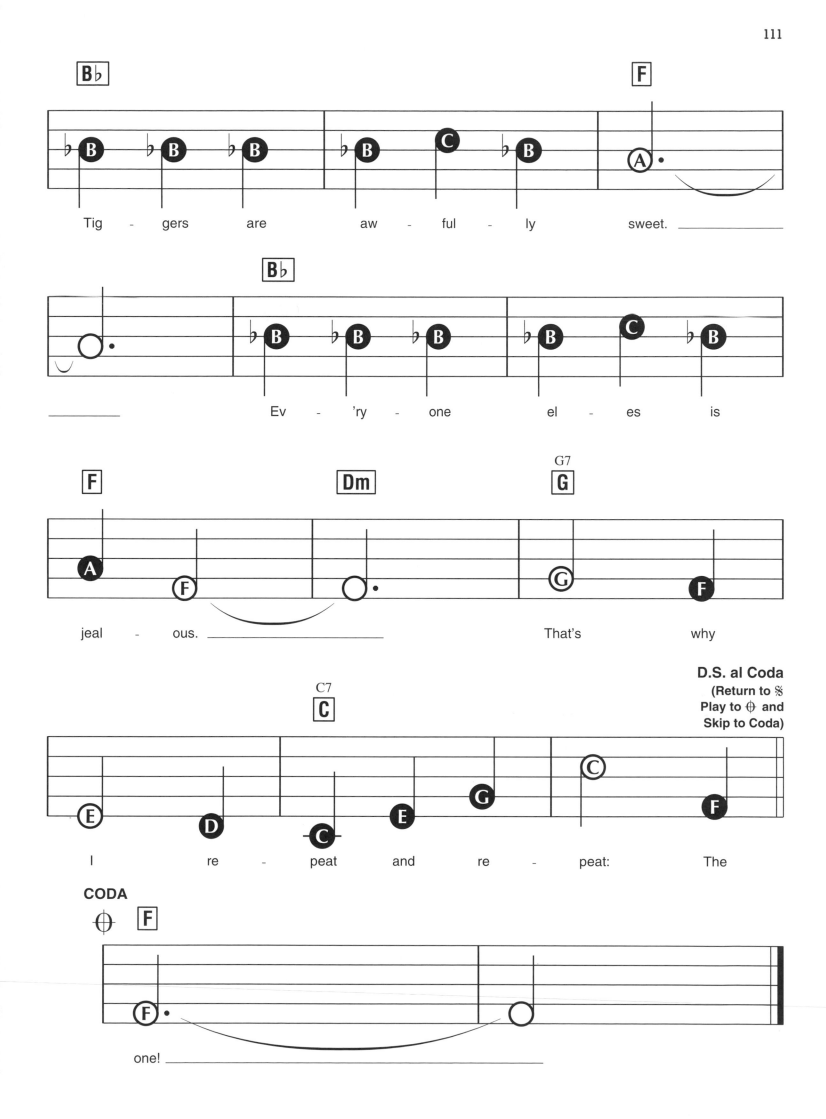

Yo Ho
(A Pirate's Life for Me)
from Disney Parks' Pirates of the Caribbean® attraction

Registration 8
Rhythm: 6/8 March

Words by Xavier Atencio
Music by George Bruns

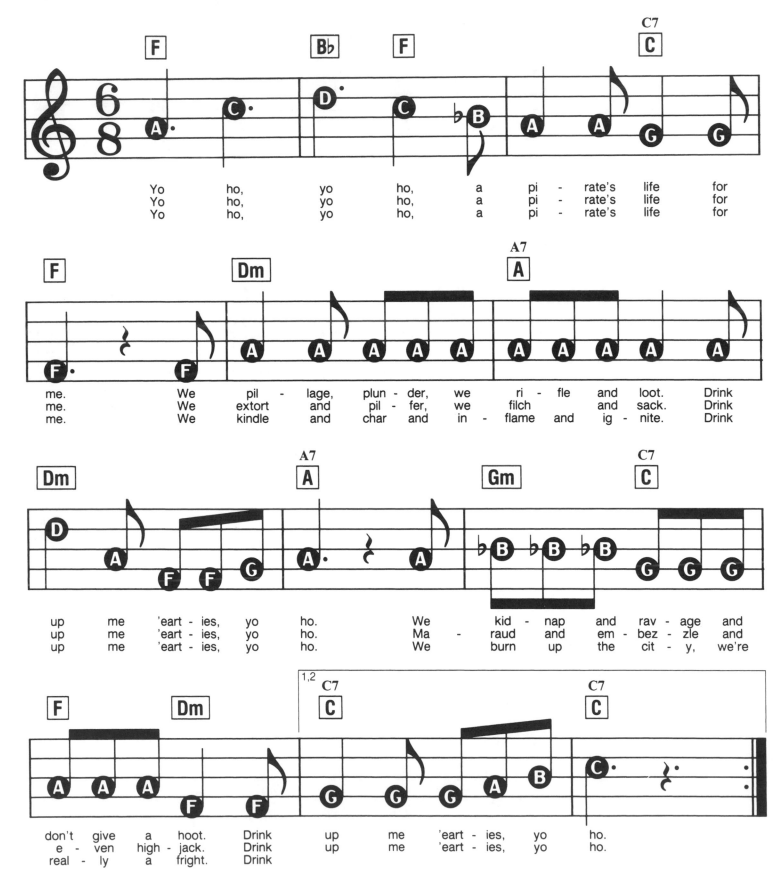

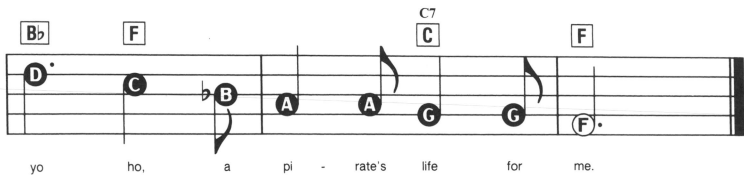

You Can Fly! You Can Fly! You Can Fly!
from PETER PAN

Registration 8
Rhythm: Fox Trot or Swing

Words by Sammy Cahn
Music by Sammy Fain

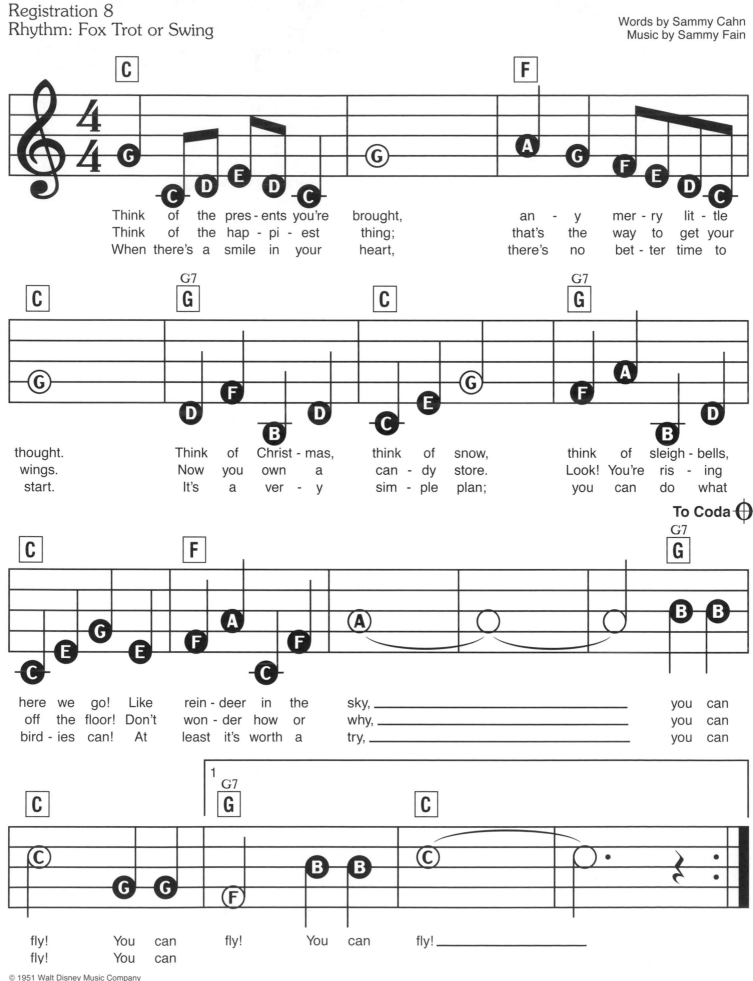

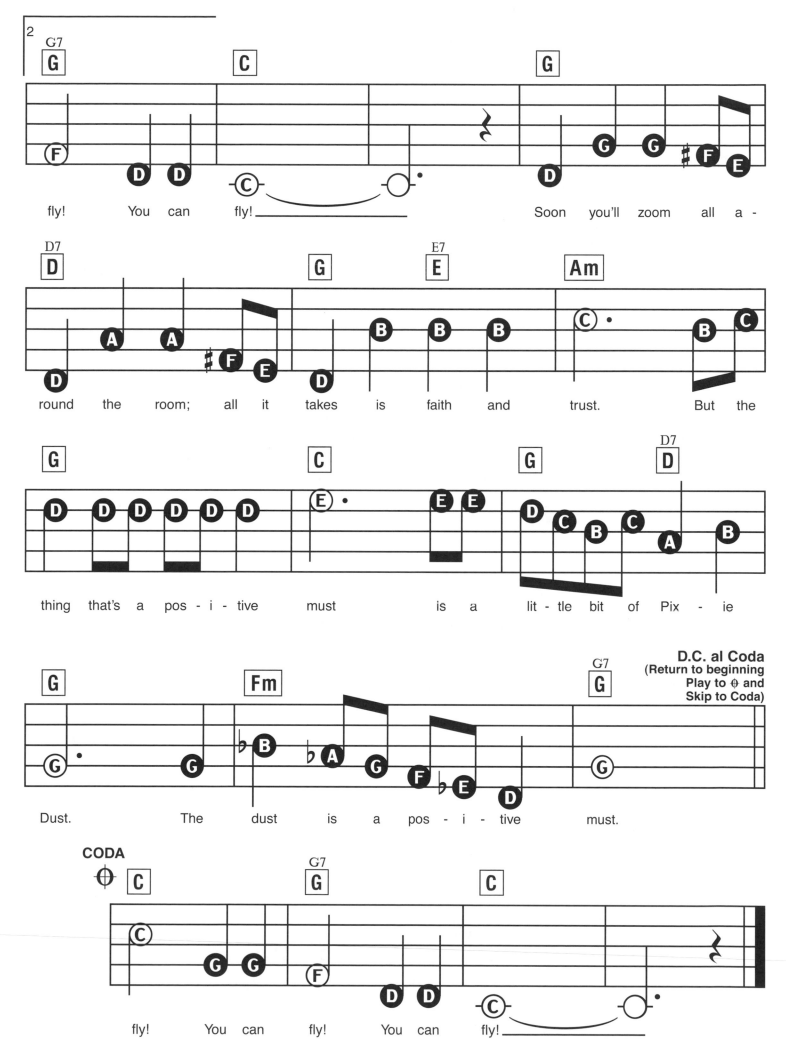

You're Welcome
from MOANA

Registration 2
Rhythm: Swing or Broadway

Music and Lyrics by
Lin-Manuel Miranda

C

G

C C C C C C

F

A

bB

MAUI: I   see   what's   hap - pen - ing   yeah: _____   You're

C7
C

bB bB bB bB bB A G F

C

E·   A C E C

face   to   face   with   great - ness,   and   it's   strange.   You   don't   e - ven

F

A G F

C

G A A

Am

A A A   bB bB

know   how   you   feel.   It's   a - dor - a - ble.   Well,   it's

C7
C

bB B B A B A G F   E   C C   C   A G E

nice   to   see   that   hu - mans   nev - er   change.   O - pen   your   eyes.   Let's   be -

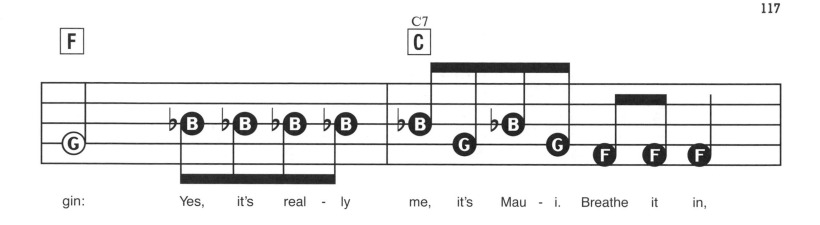

gin: Yes, it's real - ly me, it's Mau - i. Breathe it in,

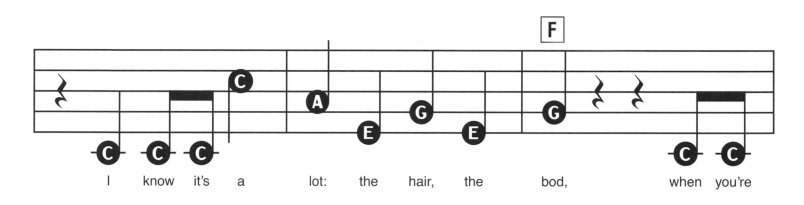

I know it's a lot: the hair, the bod, when you're

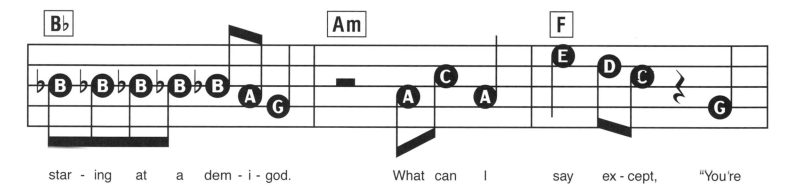

star - ing at a dem - i - god. What can I say ex - cept, "You're

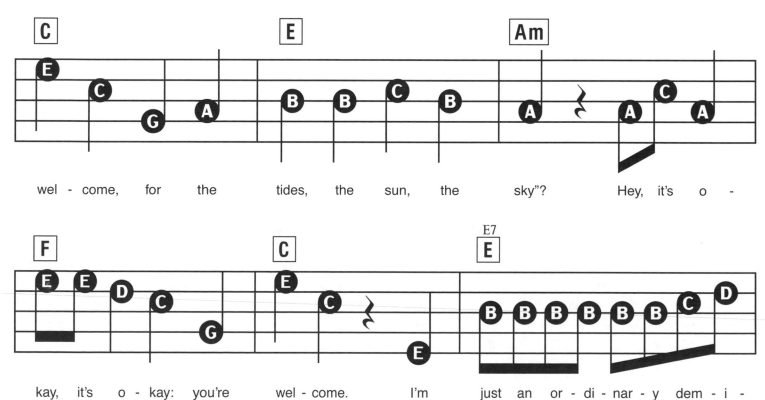

wel - come, for the tides, the sun, the sky"? Hey, it's o -

kay, it's o - kay: you're wel - come. I'm just an or - di - nar - y dem - i -

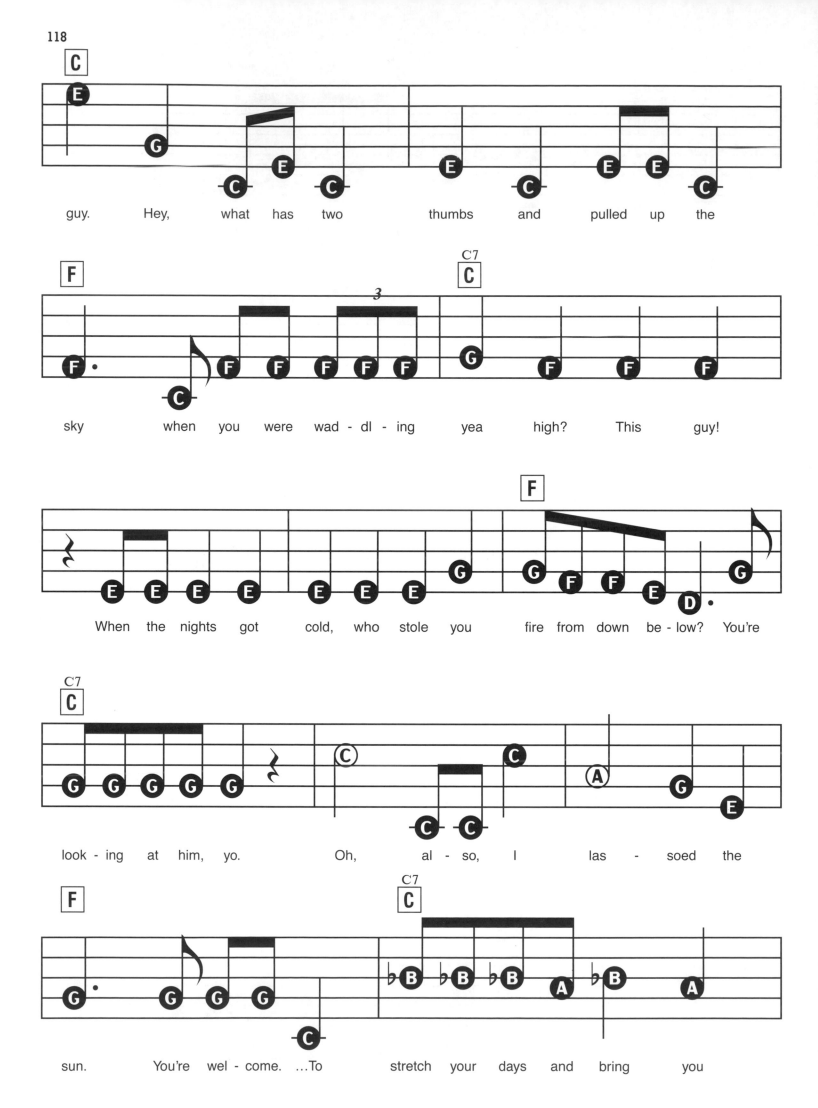

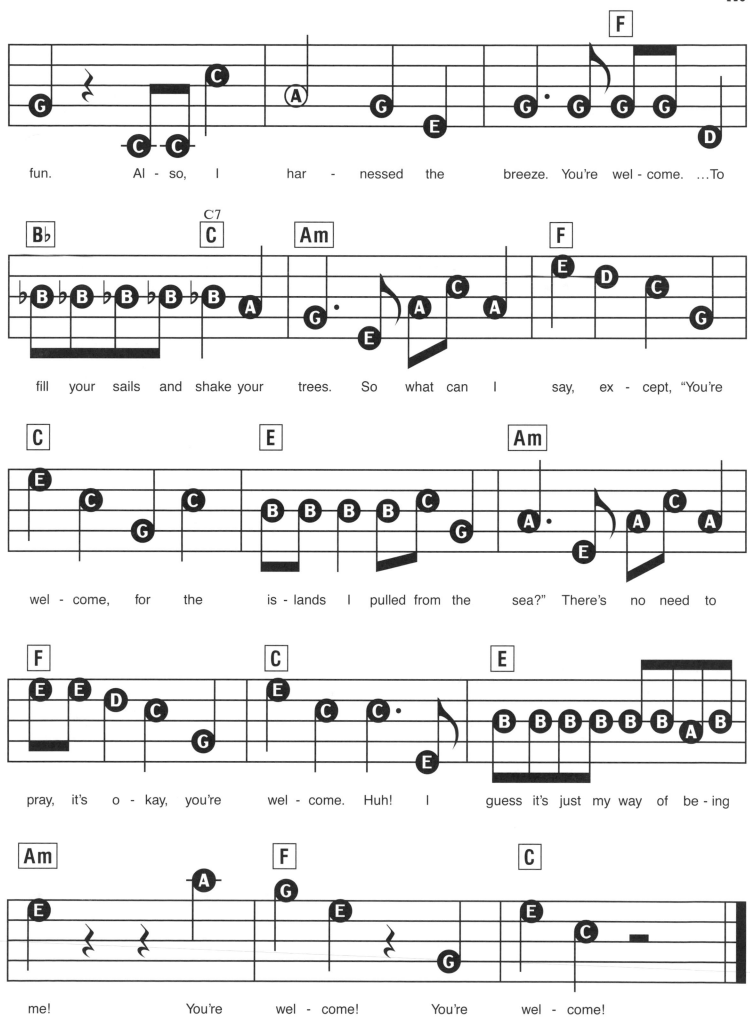

fun.   Al - so,   I   har - nessed   the   breeze.   You're wel - come. ...To

fill   your   sails   and   shake   your   trees.   So   what   can   I   say,   ex - cept, "You're

wel - come,   for   the   is - lands   I   pulled from the   sea?"   There's   no   need   to

pray,   it's   o - kay,   you're   wel - come.   Huh!   I   guess   it's   just   my   way   of   be - ing

me!   You're   wel - come!   You're   wel - come!

Zip-A-Dee-Doo-Dah
from SONG OF THE SOUTH

Registration 8
Rhythm: Fox Trot or Swing

Words by Ray Gilbert
Music by Allie Wrubel

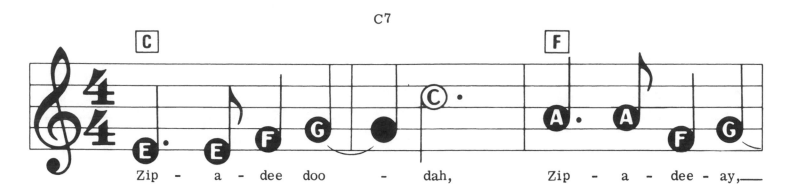

Zip - a - dee doo - dah, Zip - a - dee - ay,

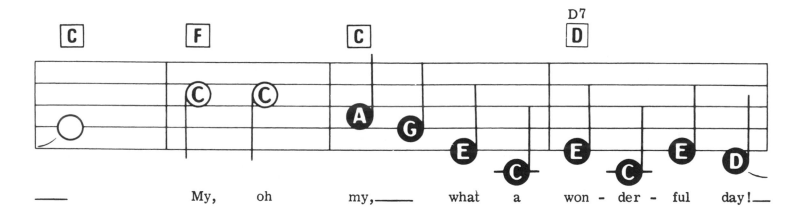

My, oh my,___ what a won-der-ful day!___

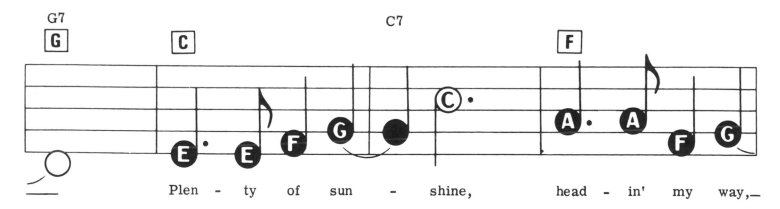

Plen - ty of sun - shine, head - in' my way,___

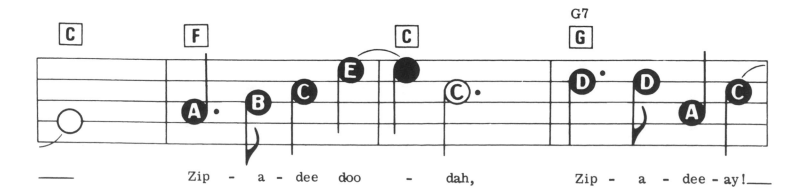

Zip - a - dee doo - dah, Zip - a - dee - ay!___

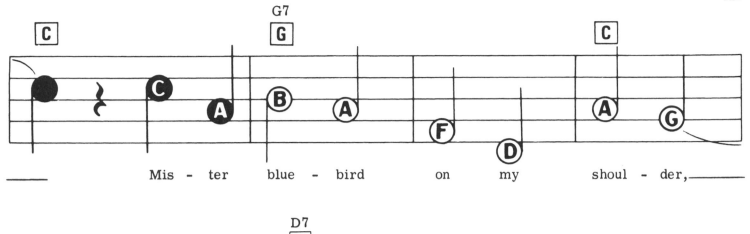

Mis - ter blue - bird on my shoul - der,_____

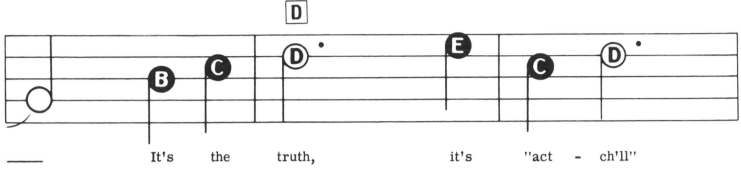

_____ It's the truth, it's "act - ch'll"

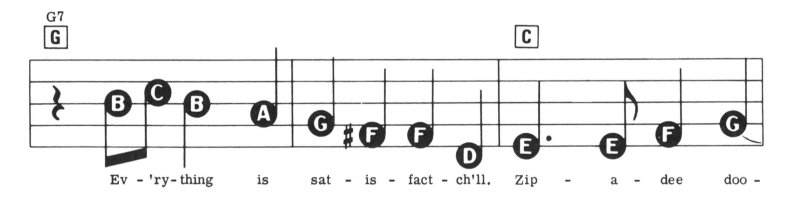

Ev - 'ry - thing is sat - is - fact - ch'll. Zip - a - dee doo -

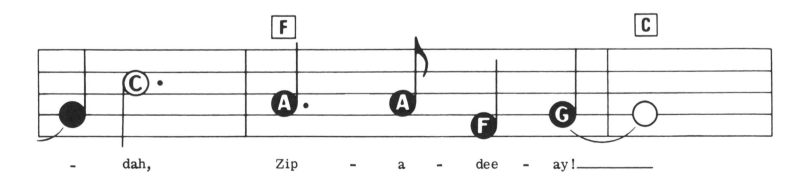

- dah, Zip - a - dee - ay!_____

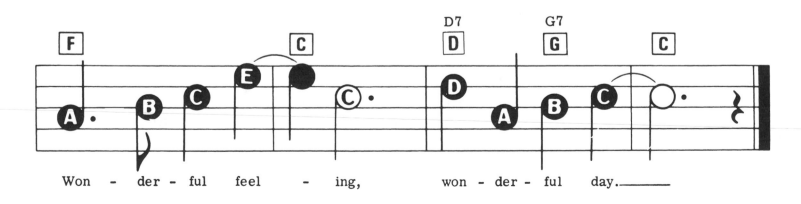

Won - der - ful feel - ing, won - der - ful day._____

You've Got a Friend in Me
from TOY STORY

Registration 7
Rhythm: Shuffle

Music and Lyrics by
Randy Newman

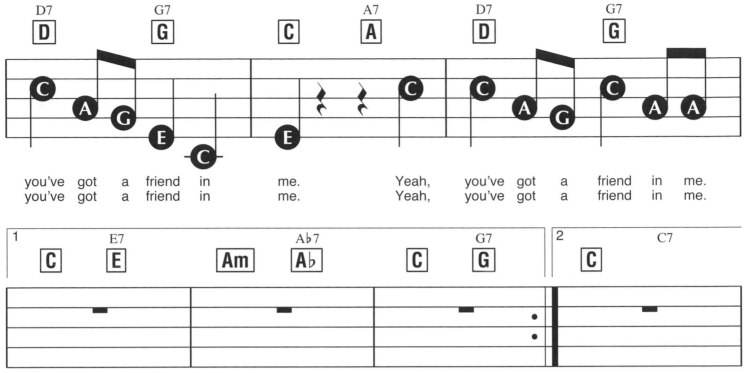

you've got a friend in me.
you've got a friend in Yeah, you've got a friend in me.

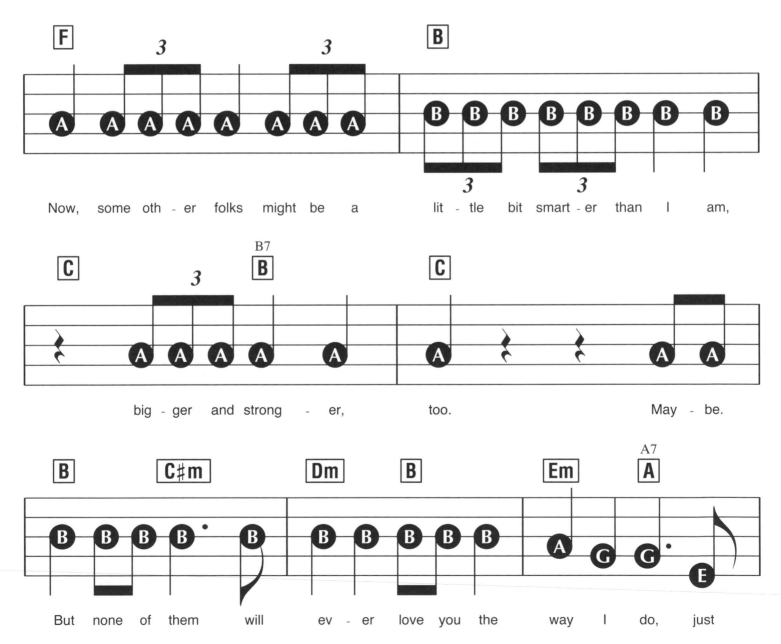

Now, some oth - er folks might be a   lit - tle bit smart - er than I am,

big - ger and strong - er,   too.   May - be.

But none of them will   ev - er love you the   way I do, just

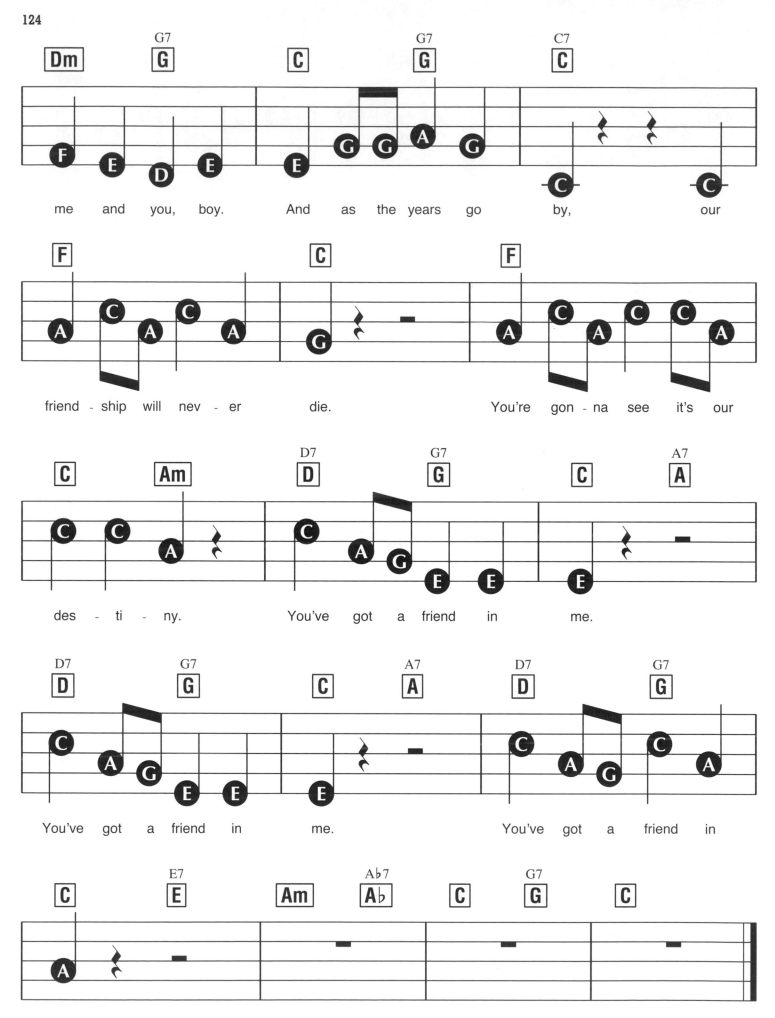

Registration Guide

• Match the Registration number on the song to the corresponding numbered category below. Select and activate an instrumental sound available on your instrument.

• Choose an automatic rhythm appropriate to the mood and style of the song. (Consult your Owner's Guide for proper operation of automatic rhythm features.)

• Adjust the tempo and volume controls to comfortable settings.

Registration

1	Mellow	Flutes, Clarinet, Oboe, Flugel Horn, Trombone, French Horn, Organ Flutes
2	Ensemble	Brass Section, Sax Section, Wind Ensemble, Full Organ, Theater Organ
3	Strings	Violin, Viola, Cello, Fiddle, String Ensemble, Pizzicato, Organ Strings
4	Guitars	Acoustic/Electric Guitars, Banjo, Mandolin, Dulcimer, Ukulele, Hawaiian Guitar
5	Mallets	Vibraphone, Marimba, Xylophone, Steel Drums, Bells, Celesta, Chimes
6	Liturgical	Pipe Organ, Hand Bells, Vocal Ensemble, Choir, Organ Flutes
7	Bright	Saxophones, Trumpet, Mute Trumpet, Synth Leads, Jazz/Gospel Organs
8	Piano	Piano, Electric Piano, Honky Tonk Piano, Harpsichord, Clavi
9	Novelty	Melodic Percussion, Wah Trumpet, Synth, Whistle, Kazoo, Perc. Organ
10	Bellows	Accordion, French Accordion, Mussette, Harmonica, Pump Organ, Bagpipes

E-Z PLAY® TODAY PUBLICATIONS

The E-Z Play® Today songbook series is the shortest distance between beginning music and playing fun! Check out this list of highlights and visit www.halleonard.com for a complete listing of all volumes and songlists.

Prices, contents, and availability subjec